PRAYING
WITH
ICONS

☦

Nuns in Kiev holding icons for an outdoor Easter procession.

PRAYING

WITH

ICONS

Jim Forest

ORBIS BOOKS

Maryknoll, New York 10545

The Catholic Foreign Mission Society of America (Maryknoll) recruits and trains people for overseas missionary service. Through Orbis Books, Maryknoll aims to foster the international dialogue that is essential to mission. The books published, however, reflect the opinions of their authors and are not meant to represent the official position of the society.

Copyright © 1997 Jim Forest

Photographs copyright © 1997 Jim Forest

Published by Orbis Books, Maryknoll, New York, U.S.A.

Manufactured in the United States of America

Library of Congress Cataloging-in-Publication Data
Forest, James H.
    Praying with icons / Jim Forest.
      p. cm.
    Includes bibliographical references.
    ISBN 1-57075-112-9 (alk. paper)
    1. Icons – Cult. 2. Icons – Cult – Meditations. 3. Catholic Church –
Prayer-books and devotions – English.   I. Title.
BX378.5.F67 1997
246'.53 – dc21   96-37303
                                                          CIP

To Nancy

✢

THE PILGRIM
There he stands
on a blue speck spinning,
a whisper of earth remaining...
and still,
everything seems possible
between the icon and the kiss.
—David Athey

Contents

Part IV
THE SAINTS

Part V
PRAYERS OF THE DAY

Acknowledgments _____

No one does anything alone. This book wouldn't have begun and certainly wouldn't have seen the light of day without the encouragement of Robert Ellsberg, editor-in-chief of Orbis Books. Learning to pray with icons has happened largely within my marriage, and so Nancy's role in this book is fundamental. Had I never met Dorothy Day or Thomas Merton, I might forever have remained indifferent to icons. Father Henri Nouwen's wedding gift to us of a print of the Holy Trinity icon and his careful explanation of much that we wouldn't have seen in it without his help is among this book's beginning points. Life within our parish in Amsterdam, St. Nicholas of Myra Russian Orthodox Church, has been another primary source; I cannot imagine this book without our two pastors, Father Alexis Voogd and Father Sergei Ovsiannikov. Still another source of stimulation, inspiration, and support is Harry Isbell, with whom I was in frequent correspondence throughout the months this book was being written.

Among people who have read this text, or parts of it, in manuscript and given helpful advice and correction, let me mention especially Doreen Bartholomew, Bob Flanagan, Maria Hamilton, Margot Muntz, Mark Pearson, Ivan Sewter, Sue and Dana Talley, and my wife, Nancy. I thank God for their patient care, assistance, and correction.

Seventeenth-century copy of the Vladimir Mother of God icon. Having gone from Russia to Jerusalem in the hands of a pilgrim, it now hangs in the author's home.

Introduction _____

In 1962 Thomas Merton sent me a postcard-sized black-and-white photograph of an icon of Mary holding the Christ child. The caption on the back indicated the original was painted in the Russian city of Novgorod in the sixteenth century. At the time I gave the image little attention. I imagined a donor had given a carton of icon prints to the Abbey of Gethsemani and Merton had decided to use them for note cards. In the months that followed other icon photos occasionally arrived, each with a message from Merton on the back. It came as a surprise years later to discover that no other form of art was more valued by Merton or had played such a significant role in his spiritual development.[1]

In my eyes at the time, icons belonged to the infancy of art, while the masterpieces of the Renaissance were what the child became. I regarded all religious art chiefly as a form of illustration or visual meditation. Though I was struggling to learn how to pray at a deeper level, longing for a more vital experience of connection with God, I never imagined icons could be helpful.

Several decades have passed since receiving that small, unvalued gift. Little by little I have found myself drawn to icons until, both in church and at home, they are at the heart of my life. Yet moving from a vague interest in icons to living with them in an intimate way took a long time.

One step along the way happened during a stay in prison in Wisconsin, a "sabbatical year" that had come about as a result of my helping burn draft records one summer afternoon in 1968 when the Vietnam War was at its height. Thanks to the link between the prison library and the state university library system, I was able to read works of Russian literature that I hadn't found time for in earlier years — first Tolstoy's novels, later Dostoevsky's. One of the most important books for me was an autobiographical work by Maxim Gorky, *My Childhood*. While Christian faith eluded Gorky in adulthood, what he wrote about his beloved and saintly grandmother provided a remarkable portrait of Orthodox religious life, including a vivid description of prayer — spoken and silent, standing and prostrate — with icons.

> Grandmother would wake up and sit for a long time on the edge of the bed combing her wonderfully long hair. With her teeth clenched she would twitch her head and tear out whole plaits of long black silky hair and curse, under her breath, so as not to wake me: "To hell with this hair! I can't do a thing with it."
>
> When she had somehow managed to disentangle her hair, she would quickly plait it into thick strands, hurriedly wash herself, snorting angrily, and then stand before her icons, without having succeeded in washing away the irritation from her large face, all wrinkled with sleep. And now would begin the real morning ablution which straightaway completely refreshed her. She would straighten her stooping back, throw her head back and gaze lovingly at the round face of the Virgin of Kazan, throw her arms out wide, cross herself fervently and whisper in a heated voice: "Blessed Virgin, remember us in times of trouble!"
>
> She would bow down to the floor, slowly unbend and then whisper again ardently: "Source of all joys, purest beauty, flowering apple tree...." Almost every morning she would find some new words of praise, which made me listen to her prayers with even greater attention.
>
> "Dearest heart of heaven, my refuge and protection, Golden Sun, Mother of God, save us from evil, grant we offend no one, and that I, in turn, be not offended without just cause!"
>
> Her dark eyes smiled and she seemed to grow younger again as she crossed herself again with slow movements of her heavy hand.
>
> "Jesus Christ, Son of God, be merciful to me, poor sinner, for Thine own Mother's sake."[2]

I read those pages again and again, envying Gorky his grandmother and the lost culture she belonged to — at least I assumed it was lost, buried beneath the Gulag Archipelago. Only many years later did I begin to realize that women like Gorky's beloved grandmother were alive and praying in much the same way. How perceptive was Gorky's portrait of fundamentals of Orthodox spirituality: the seamless integration of spiritual and physical action; the emphasis on praise; the recognition of pure beauty as a revelation of God; and the particular gratitude for Mary, who became the gateway of the Incarnation and the mother of the Church.

Another event which helped me to understand icons happened in the late seventies in Belgium, several years after my work had brought me to Holland to head the staff of the International Fellowship of Reconciliation. I had been taking part in a small conference in Antwerp. During the pause in the meeting, I took Father Elias Chacour, a priest from Galilee, to see the house of the seventeenth-century artist Peter Paul Rubens. It was one of the city's best preserved ancient houses — one could imagine that Rubens might be back at any moment.

Toward the end of our visit we were standing in front of a large painting of the parting of the Red Sea and I was waiting for Father Elias to tell me what he thought of it. Finally he confessed, "It's too noisy." In a flash I realized that, yes, it was a painting with a Cecil B. De Mille soundtrack. You could hear the waters parting, hear Moses shouting words of encouragement, even hear the cries of Pharaoh's drowning soldiers as the sea rushed back in again in defense of the escaping Jews. It was amazing people didn't go deaf standing near such a canvas.

The idea that a painting might be described in terms of sound levels was new to me. Implied in what Father Elias said was the thought that a painting might also communicate levels of silence, and that it might be certain kinds of silence one searched for in art.

A year or two later, while staying with friends in Birmingham, England, I visited the Barber Institute, a small art museum with a collection of masterpieces arranged in chronological order. Item number one was a Byzantine icon that was eight centuries old. I still can feel the surprise that swept over me as I was drawn into that icon's blessed silence. Though I eagerly looked forward to seeing other paintings I had glimpsed on entering the gallery — Renoir, van Gogh, Matisse, Chagall — it was hard to go further. The most remarkable thing was that the icon made me want to pray.

Then came a second revelation, the understanding that the anonymous person whose work was before me (icons are unsigned; rarely is it known who made a particular icon) would have been grieved to know his much prayed-over panel had ended up in a place so detached from worship; not that one can't pray in a museum, but the icon couldn't be kissed nor illuminated by a candle, the usual light source for an icon. A museum encourages none of the gestures, the body language, that from a traditional Christian viewpoint go along with icons and are inseparable from prayer.

The next major step for me was my first trip to Russia in the fall of 1983. In Moscow I witnessed again and again the way Orthodox Christians live with icons, responding to them with an intimacy and warmth that filled me with wonder and appreciation — not to mention a certain envy, as I could hardly imagine myself being as free, wholehearted, and expressive in prayer as they were. There seemed to be no border between physical and spiritual life.

Icons, I began to understand, while helping make the church building more beautiful, were far more than decorations and also more than a non-verbal teaching device, a Bible for the illiterate, as was sometimes explained with condescension. Icons helped to erase borders of time and space. They helped me sense the closeness rather than the remoteness of the events and people portrayed. Even when there was no Liturgy in progress, the activity of prayer, much of it connected with icons, filled the church. People stopping at particular icons often seemed to be greeting dear friends. The candles that were flickering throughout the church were equal to the number of kisses that had been bestowed on icons.

I overheard someone say in English, "A pretty sight — a pity it's all idolatry." Yet it was obvious that icons themselves were not being worshiped, but were serving as points of connection with Christ and the community of saints. Of course Christ and the saints are close with or without icons, but one could see how icons help to overcome all that normally impedes our

awareness that we live in the presence of God and in the midst ✗
of a "cloud of witnesses."

Still, I remained a bystander for several more years, even
though we were living with a wonderful reproduction of the
Holy Trinity icon that Henri Nouwen had given us as a wedding gift. It had a place of honor in our home and certainly
added something helpful to the atmosphere of daily life, but
the place where it hung wasn't yet a locus of prayer.

Then came the spring of 1985 when I had a three-month
sabbatical from my work with the International Fellowship of
Reconciliation. Providentially, I had been invited to teach and
study at the Ecumenical Institute at Tantur, a Vatican-sponsored
center for research and interfaith dialogue near Bethlehem on
the road from Jerusalem.

A small hope that Nancy and I brought with us was that we
might find a hand-painted icon in Jerusalem, and we did. On
our very first day in the Old City, in the window of a dingy
shop near the Jaffa Gate, a small icon of Mary and the Christ
Child caught our eye. It was a hundred dollars, the Palestinian
owner told us — not much for an icon, but at the time it seemed
more than we could afford. We hesitated, and not only because
of our meager financial resources. Other shops in Jerusalem
were full of icons, though even our untrained eyes could see
that most of them were hastily painted mass-production jobs
that had been "aged" in ovens. We decided not to hurry, yet
week after week we looked with gratitude at that one haunting
icon whenever we passed the shop — until one day it was gone,
and then we grieved.

A week later I went into the shop and asked the owner if he
might have anything similar. "Similar! I have the very icon. No
one wanted it so I took it out of the window." He quickly found
it. Asking him to keep it for me, I gave him a ten dollar bill and
the next day returned with the rest. I wrapped the icon in a
freshly washed diaper (Anne was still a baby) and took it back
to Tantur.

Graced by that small icon, our apartment became a different
place. I remember carefully unwrapping it and Nancy lighting
a candle. What better way to receive an icon than to pray? That
was clear. But what prayers? We recited the Te Deum from the

Anglican Book of Common Prayer. We read Mary's Magnificat. Just a few days before we had bought a Jewish prayer book and easily found several suitable prayers addressed to the Creator of the Universe. We recited the text of the Litany of Peace used in the Liturgy of St. John Chrysostom.[3] We sang a Protestant hymn Nancy knew from her childhood, growing up in the Dutch Reformed Church. Never was there a more hodge-podge service, such an awkward, Marx Brothers beginning; but whatever the moment lacked in grace was more than made up for in gratitude.

Later we showed the icon to a Roman Catholic priest who admired the Orthodox Church and was well-versed in icons. It was Russian, he told us, and had the name "the Vladimir Mother of God" because the prototype had for many years been in the Russian city of Vladimir. He guessed ours was three hundred years old, possibly more. "Tens of thousands of Russian pilgrims came to Jerusalem in the nineteenth century, many of them walking most of the way," he said. "Probably one of them brought this along and it never found its way back to Russia." He told us it was worth far more than we had paid for it and could only have come to us as a gift of the Mother of God.

Whether he was right about the age of the icon, its provenance, or its material worth to collectors, I have no idea. It doesn't matter. What he was certainly right about was that it was Mary's gift to us.

Later that year, when we were back in Holland, Nancy had a dream which we both received as another gift from God. We still talk about it from time to time. Here is Nancy's account of what she experienced:

> I was traveling on a raft down a stream that cut through the landscape. The level of the water was very low and the banks of the stream were high, so that standing on the raft I couldn't actually see above the steep embankments on either side of the stream. It was a bright summer day. But I could hear the sounds of bombs exploding on either side of the stream, and I could see bright flashes in the air, the same bright flashes that nuclear weapons produce. I was passing through a battle zone.

There were several other people on the raft. I don't know who they were. But as we moved slowly down the stream through the terrible explosions, I was struck with the realization that if we on the raft would just maintain a silent, peaceful calm, we would make it down the stream to safety. So I tried to calm down my fellow passengers, mostly by my own example. I stood on the raft, facing ahead in the direction that it was moving, and suddenly there at the bow of the raft appeared the icon of the Savior. I realized that if we would fix our gaze on that icon and breathe slowly and calmly and, above all, remain still, we would get through the battle zone.

It was a tremendously calming dream, and it has continued to instruct me ever since. While the dream occurred at a time when there was a widespread sense of the immediate danger of nuclear war, my life continues to be studded with the terrors that any conscious person has to live with. But the truth of that dream — that we are traveling down through time, and that we must fix our gaze on Christ — is always there.

The next day we found a postcard reproduction of the icon she had dreamed about — it was the Savior of Zvenigorod, also sometimes called Christ the Peacemaker, a fifteenth-century icon by St. Andrei Rublev that was nearly destroyed after the Bolshevik Revolution. (*See color section.*) Most of the original image was lost except for Christ's face. Nancy hung it on the wall over our bed. It has been in our bedroom ever since.

Soon after her dream a visitor brought us as a gift a small hand-painted icon of the Savior. It was of Greek origin, though he had found it in Rome. It became part of our icon corner.

More than a decade has passed. If I am not traveling, my days begin and end in front of our icon from Jerusalem plus the others that gradually have found their way to us. Every night before Nancy and I go to bed, we say our prayers together before our icon shelf, using traditional Orthodox prayers we have learned by heart since being received into the Orthodox Church in 1988.

Occasionally it crosses my mind that I may have our Mary

icon before my eyes when I am facing death — a comforting thought. Other times I worry that it will be stolen, or that our house will burn and our icons with it. Then I remember such losses aren't so important. I would miss the small image of Mary and Christ that came to us in 1985, but it has become so much a part of me that there is no way I can be separated from it. Also each icon has countless sister icons and only a very attentive eye can tell them apart. Truly, no icon can be lost.

JIM FOREST
Feast of St. Ephraim the Syrian
February 10, 1996

Part I

In the Image of God

☦

Wood panels being prepared for use as icon
surfaces in the studio of Father Zinon.

A Short History of Icons

He is the image [in Greek, ikon] *of the invisible God, the firstborn of all creation.*

— COLOSSIANS 1:15

"I have seen a great many portraits of the Savior, and of Peter and Paul, which have been preserved up to our time," Eusebius recorded in his *History of the Church* early in the fourth century.[4] While visiting Caesarea Philippi in Galilee, he also noted seeing a centuries-old bronze statue of the Savior outside the house of the woman who had been cured of incessant bleeding by Christ. His witness is all the more compelling as Eusebius was one of those who regarded religious images as belonging more to the pagan world than to the Church.

According to legend, the first icon was made when King Abgar of Osroene, dying of leprosy, sent a message begging Jesus to visit him in Edessa and cure him. Hurrying toward Jerusalem and his Crucifixion, Christ instead sent a healing gift. He pressed his face against a linen cloth, making the square of fabric bear his image. The miraculous icon remained in Edessa until the tenth century, when it was brought to Constantinople. Then, after the city was sacked by the Crusaders in 1204, it disappeared altogether. Known as "Not Made by Human Hands" or the "Holy Face," the icon has often been reproduced down to our own day. A recently made copy from Russia is on the desk in front of me as I write this book. (*See color section.*)

In the Western Church a similar story is associated with the name of Veronica, one of the women who comforted Jesus as he was bearing the cross. She offered him a cloth to wipe the blood and sweat from his face and afterward found she had received a miraculous image. A building along the Via Dolorosa associated with Veronica is today home to a community of the Little Sisters of Jesus who, appropriately, support themselves by selling icon prints mounted on olive wood.

3

The Apostle and Evangelist Luke is regarded as the first to have painted an icon. (In the Orthodox Church, it is often said that an icon is written rather than painted but in this text I use what seems the plainer term.) St. Luke is credited with three icons of Mary, in one case using the wood of the table where Christ's mother and St. John ate their meals. The best known is "Our Lady of Tenderness" in which the face of the child Jesus is pressing his face against his mother's. Another, the "Hodigitria," has a more formal arrangement, showing Mary presenting her son to the viewer; it is known as "She Who Shows the Way." Finally Luke painted an icon of Mary in prayer, with outstretched arms, an image sometimes seen in Orthodox churches in the sanctuary above the altar. The placing of the icon near the altar serves as a reminder that Mary became the bridge linking heaven and earth.

Several ancient icons bear layer upon layer of paint as later iconographers restored work that had become too dark or too damaged with the passage of time. Perhaps at the foundation level of one or another ancient icon are brush strokes that were made by the hand of St. Luke. Or perhaps not. Nearly all ancient icons were destroyed either during times of persecution in the first three centuries of the Christian era or during the iconoclastic periods in the eighth and ninth centuries.

Fortunately there are many Christian images from the age of martyrs that have survived, most notably in the Roman Catacombs and burial houses but also in many other places, from Asia Minor to Spain. These frescoes are simple and sober images, made with few brush strokes and a narrow range of colors, with such subjects as Christ carrying a lamb, the three young men praising God from within a furnace, the raising of Lazarus, and the eucharistic meal. The Catacombs bear witness that wherever Christians prayed, they sought to create a visual environment that reminded them of the Kingdom of God and helped them to pray.

Many early icons of a more developed style survive in Rome, though they are chiefly mosaics and thus have a monumental aspect, a type of public Christian art that only became possible after the age of persecution ended. In one of Rome's earliest principal churches, Santa Maria Maggiore, there are mosaics from the fourth century, but, as they are high up on the walls, you need binoculars to appreciate them. The large and vivid fifth-century mosaic icons above and behind the altar, however, are easy to see and deeply moving. Among other Roman churches that contain impressive examples of iconography from the first millennium of Christianity are Sts. Cosmas and Damian, St. John Lateran, Santa Sabina, Santa Constanza, San Clemente, Santa Prassede, Santa Agnese fuori le Mura, Santa Maria in Trastevere, and San Paolo fuori le Mura.[5]

Many early icons also survive in the monastery of St. Catherine at the foot of Mount Sinai. Here we find icon portraits of both Christ and the Apostle Peter. Art historians date these from the sixth and seventh centuries. Both have an almost photographic realism. The style has much in common with Roman and Egyptian portraiture of classical times. They are probably similar to the icons mentioned by Eusebius.

Even if no original icon from the apostolic age has survived, one is impressed to see how, generation after generation, devout iconographers have sought to make faithful copies of earlier icons, a process that continues to the present day. Thus images of Christ and the Apostles are recognizable from century to century despite occasional changes in style. We know, for example, that Peter had thick curly hair while Paul was bald. Most important, the memory of Christ's face is preserved.

Just as in our own time there is controversy about icons, so was there dispute in the early Church. Early critics of icons included Tertullian, Clement of Alexandria, Minucius Felix, and Lactantius. Eusebius was not alone in fearing that the art of the pagan world carried with it the spirit of the pagan world, while others objected on the basis of Old Testament restrictions of imagery. Christianity was, after all, born in a world in which many artists were employed doing religious, political, and secular work. Idolatry was a normal part of pagan religious life. Thus we find that in the early centuries, in the many areas of controversy among Christians, there was division on questions of religious art and its place in spiritual life. It is instructive to notice that those who were reluctant to accept that Christ was God incarnate were also resistant to icons.

At the heart of all theological dispute, from that time into our own day, stands the question: Who is Jesus Christ?

Some argued that Jesus was simply a man of such exemplary goodness that he was adopted by God as Son. Going further with this idea, others believed God so overwhelmed Jesus the Galilean that his manhood was gradually absorbed into divinity. There were those who argued that Jesus merely appeared to be a person of human flesh but was in reality pure spirit; flesh being subject to passions, illness, and decay, they argued that God could never inhabit flesh.

Orthodoxy's answer — that in the womb of Mary the Second Person of the Holy Trinity became a human being, thus that Jesus was both true God and true man — was both too simple and too radical for many people. How could the all-powerful God clothe divinity in that which can suffer death and corruption?

Discussion of this issue and its implications constituted the center point for the Church's Ecumenical Councils. Though we find the Orthodox teaching already expressed in the creed of the first Ecumenical Council, in Nicea in 325, still it took centuries for the Church to shake off the influence of heresies which, in a variety of ways, denied the Incarnation. In fact, as we see in the churches today, the same arguments continue.

Each Church assembly which affirmed the icon was affirming the Incarnation. For example, the Quinisext Council in Trullo, in 692, while condemning "deceitful paintings that corrupt the intelligence by exciting shameful pleasures," recognized the icon as a mirror of grace and truth. "In order to expose to the sight of all what is perfect," the Council declared, "even with the help of painting, we decide that henceforth Christ our God must be presented in his human form."

The argument over icons reached its boiling point in the eighth and ninth centuries at the time when Islam was rapidly spreading in areas that had formerly been Christian. In 725 Emperor Leo III, ignoring the opposition of both Patriarch Germanus of Constantinople and Pope Gregory II in Rome, ordered the removal of icons from the churches and their destruction. He may have hoped his order would help stop the spread of Islam, which was firmly opposed to images in places of worship.

Painting by Turligin shows a monk painting an icon
during the period of iconoclasm, when iconographers
were imprisoned and tortured.

Many iconographers from the Byzantine world fled to Italy, finding protection from the pope. It was a period in which many who upheld Orthodox belief suffered loss of property, imprisonment, beatings, and mutilation.

Some iconoclasts argued that images of Christ, representing as they did his physical appearance, diminished his divinity by revealing only his humanity. One beneficial consequence of the iconoclastic movement was that makers of icons searched for better ways to represent in paint the hidden, spiritual reality rather than merely the physical aspects of the person represented.

The theologian who best defended the use of icons in Christian life was St. John of Damascus (676–749), a monk and poet kept safe from the power of the iconoclastic emperor through ironic circumstances — his monastery, Mar Saba, in the desert southeast of Jerusalem, was in an area under Islamic rule, out of reach of imperial edict. Here he wrote his essay "On the Divine Images" in which he reasoned:

> If we made an image of the invisible God, we would certainly be in error... but we do not do anything of the kind; we do not err, in fact, if we make the image of God incarnate who appeared on earth in the flesh, who in his ineffable goodness, lived with men and assumed the nature, the volume, the form, and the color of the flesh.

St. John also responded to the arguments of those who regarded Old Testament prohibitions of religious imagery as also applying to the Church:

> Since the invisible One became visible by taking on flesh, you can fashion the image of him whom you saw. Since he who has neither body nor form nor quantity nor quality, who goes beyond all grandeur by the excellence of his nature, he, being of divine nature, took on the condition of a slave and reduced himself to quantity and quality by clothing himself in human features. Therefore, paint on wood and present for contemplation him who desired to become visible.[6]

The first iconoclastic period lasted fifty-five years, until 780. Seven years later, at the Seventh Ecumenical Council, the bishops rose in defense of the icon. The Council affirmed that it is not the icon itself which is venerated but the prototype whose image is represented in the icon. Iconoclasm was formally condemned.

Nonetheless, a second iconoclastic period, less severe than the first, was initiated by Emperor Leo V in 813. Orthodox resistance included an impressive act of civil disobedience — an icon-bearing procession in Constantinople by a thousand monks. With the death of Emperor Theophilus in 842, imperial objections to icons ended. In 843, Theodora, widow of the former emperor, who herself possessed icons, convened a Council which reaffirmed the teaching of the Seven Ecumenical Councils and confirmed the place of the icon in Christian life. The first Sunday of Great Lent was set aside henceforth to celebrate the Triumph of Orthodoxy, a custom maintained to the present day in the Orthodox world when the faithful bring their home icons to the church. One of the texts sung on the Sunday of Orthodoxy declares:

> The uncircumscribed Word of the Father became circumscribed, taking flesh from thee, O Mother of God, and He has restored the sullied image to its ancient glory, filling it with the divine beauty. This our salvation we confess in deed and word, and we depict it in the holy icons.

If in Byzantium the encounter with Islam initially had a devastating effect on icons, further north the Tartar invasion and occupation of the thirteenth and fourteenth centuries was to have a disruptive impact on every aspect of religious life among the Russian people, themselves latecomers to Christianity, their conversion having begun in Kiev at the end of the tenth century. Very little iconography of the first few centuries of Christian culture in Russia survives. But from the late fourteenth to the mid-sixteenth centuries, iconography was to reach heights in Russia that many regard as unparalleled before or since. The most renowned figure of the period is St. Andrei Rublev, first noted in 1405 while working in a cathedral of the Moscow Kremlin as a student of the master iconographer Theophanes the Greek. In 1425 St. Andrei painted the Holy Trinity icon, widely regarded as the highest achievement in iconographic art. St. Andrei's other masterpieces include the Savior of Zvenigorod, remarkable for the profound sense of love and mercy communicated in Christ's face.[7]

For generations Russia was a paradise of iconographic art characterized by simplicity of line, vivid and harmonious colors, grace of gesture, an amazing freshness and transparency. But in the mid-sixteenth century one begins to notice signs of decay. Complexity of design begins to take the place of simplicity while colors become duller and darker. Russian art historians attribute the change, at least in part, to the influence of prints being imported from the West. By the seventeenth century the process was well advanced. "Decline was the result of a deep spiritual crisis, a secularization of religious consciousness," writes the iconographer and scholar Leonid Ouspensky, "thanks to which, despite the vigorous opposition of the Church [which ordered the destruction of icons influenced by the artistic methods of the Renaissance], there began the penetration not merely of separate elements but of the very principles of religious art."[8]

Speeding the process of secularization was Tsar Peter the Great (1672–1725). He avidly promoted imitation of all things Western in every field, including church architecture and religious art, a process carried further by his successors. By the middle of the eighteenth century few painted icons in the traditional way, nor was such work welcomed in many churches. Traditional iconography was replaced by third-rate imitation of second-rate Western religious painting — "caricatures of icons," as Bishop Ignaty Brianchaninov, a nineteenth-century Russian prelate, remarked.[9]

Peter the Great abolished the office of Patriarch of Moscow; afterward the Russian Orthodox Church was treated as a department of government. State control lasted until the abdication of Tsar Nicholas II in 1917 — and then came the Bolshevik Revolution and a period of persecution such as Christianity hadn't experienced since Diocletian. Not only were countless icons destroyed, but millions of Orthodox believers perished as well.

It was not only in Russia that iconographers turned toward Western approaches to religious art. Similar influences were at work in other Orthodox countries. As a result, today one finds in many Orthodox churches in almost any country an odd mixture of classic iconography and much that, at best, can be appreciated only for its sincerity and, at worst, dismissed as suitable only for the basement.

Thanks largely to the uncovering and restoration of many ancient icons, the past hundred years have witnessed a gradual rebirth of appreciation of classic iconography. Today one finds good reproductions of iconographic masterpieces, not only in churches but in homes and even in offices. But it is not only a matter of reproductions. Increasingly, talented iconographers are being trained in traditional methods and in the spiritual life that sustains iconography. The result is that good hand-painted icons are becoming more common.

Qualities of the Icon

It is the task of the iconographer to open our eyes to the actual presence of the Kingdom in the world and to remind us that though we see nothing of its splendid liturgy, we are, if we believe in Christ the Redeemer, in fact living and worshiping as "fellow citizens of the angels and saints, built upon the chief cornerstone with Christ." [10]

— Thomas Merton

There are no words nor colors nor lines which could represent the Kingdom of God as we represent and describe our world. Both theology and iconography are faced with a problem which is absolutely insoluble — to express by means belonging to the created world that which is infinitely above the creature. On this plane there are no successes, for the subject itself is beyond comprehension and no matter how lofty in content and beautiful an icon may be, it cannot be perfect, just as no word or image can be perfect. In this sense both theology and iconography are always failures. Precisely in this failure lies the value of both alike; for this value results from the fact that both theology and iconography reach the limit of human possibilities and prove insufficient. Therefore the methods used by iconography for pointing to the Kingdom of God can only be figurative, symbolical, like the language of the parables in the Holy Scriptures. [11]

— Leonid Ouspensky

It is the faith of the praying person that matters most, not the quality of the icon, a lesson I learned from Dorothy Day, founder of the Catholic Worker movement. In her sixties at the time, she was having increasing trouble climbing the five flights to her apartment on Spring Street in lower Manhattan's Little Italy. A small apartment in a similar tenement on Ridge Street was rented for her; it was only one flight up, but was in appalling condition. A friend and I went down to clean and paint the two rooms. We dragged box after box of debris down to the street, including what seemed to us a hideous painting of the Holy Family. Mary, Joseph, and Jesus had been rendered in a few bright colors against a grey background on a piece of plywood. We shook our heads, deposited it in the trash along the curb, and went back to our labor. Dorothy arrived not long after, the painting in hand. "Look what I found! The Holy Family! It's a providential sign, a blessing." She put it on the mantel of the apartment's bricked-up fireplace. Looking at it again, this time I saw it was a work of love. While this primitive icon was no masterpiece, the faith of its maker shined through. But I wouldn't have seen it if Dorothy hadn't seen it first.

Let me add that Dorothy was far from unappreciative of a finely painted icon. She greatly admired those belonging to her Russian friend Helene Iswolsky and treasured a book of reproductions of the iconography of St. Andrei Rublev.

"Rublev's Holy Trinity icon," a monk told me during one of my early visits in Russia, "is a proof of God." This is a way of saying that beauty itself bears witness to God. But who can describe beauty in words? It is a futile errand to try to define what makes a good icon. It becomes still more difficult to draw the border between good iconography and that which is second-rate or simply bad.

Nonetheless certain general comments about what to look for in iconography may be helpful to those who are new to icons.

No less than the written word, an icon is an instrument for the transmission of Christian tradition and faith. Through sacred imagery, the Holy Spirit speaks to us, revealing truths that may not be evident to those using only the tools of reason.

Icons are an aid to worship. Wherever an icon is set, that place more easily becomes an area of prayer. The icon is not an end in itself but assists us in going beyond what can be seen with our physical eyes into the realm of mystical experience. "The icon," Paul Evdokimov comments, "is the last arrow of human eros shot at the heart of the mystery."[12]

The icon has a hieratic character; it is concerned solely with the sacred. Through line and color, the iconographer seeks to convey the awesomeness of the invisible and divine reality and to lead the viewer to a consciousness of the divine presence. The icon is theology written in images and color.

The icon is a work of tradition. Just as the hands of many thousands of bakers stand behind each loaf of homemade bread, the icon is more than the personal meditation of an individual artist, but the fruit of many generations of believers uniting us to the witnesses of the Resurrection.

The icon is not intended to force an emotional response. There is a conscious avoidance of movement or theatrical gesture. In portraying moments of biblical history, the faces of participants in the scene are rarely expressive of their feelings at the time as we might imagine them, but suggest virtues — purity, patience in suffering, forgiveness, compassion, and love. In Crucifixion icons, the physical pain Christ endured on the cross is not shown; the icon reveals what led him to the cross, the free action of giving his life for others. There is no superficial or exaggerated drama.

Icons guard against overfamiliarity with the divine. For example, a Savior icon is not merely a sentimental painting of "our dear friend Jesus" but portrays both his divinity as well as his manhood, his absolute demands on us as well as his infinite mercy.

The icon is silent. No mouths are open nor are there any other physical details which suggest sound. But the silence is not empty. St. Ignatius, bishop of Antioch, the disciple of St. John the Evangelist, who was martyred in Rome in the year 107, made the comment: "He who possesses in truth the word of Jesus can hear even its silence." The stillness and silence of the icon, in the home no less than church, creates an area that constantly invites prayer. The deep and living silence which marks a good icon is nothing less than the silence of Christ. It is the very opposite of the icy stillness of the tomb. It is the silence of Mary's contemplative heart, the silence of the Transfiguration, the silence of the Resurrection, the silence of the Incarnate Word.

Icons avoid artistic techniques intended to create an illusion of three-dimensional space; they suggest space without attempting to escape the plane of the panel. Even slight violations of this plane always damage the icon's meaning, much as a spoken word violates pantomime. The lighting within an icon is never explained by a single light source; light is within the image as well as exterior to it and illumines whoever stands before the icon.

The image is reduced to a minimum of detail. There is either nothing at all in the background or, if a setting is required, it is rendered in the simplest, most austere manner, often in inverse perspective in which there is no single vanishing point and in which objects often expand where, according to the rules of perspective, they should contract. Lines move *toward* rather than away from the person at prayer before the icon.[13]

Because nothing in our world can do better than hint at the beauty of the kingdom of God, natural objects are rendered in a vivid but symbolic, at times abstract, manner. "Spiritual reality cannot be represented in any other way except through symbols," noted Leonid Ouspensky. "To indicate that baptism is the entry into new life, the baptized, even a fully grown man, is represented as a small child."[14]

The icon is unsigned. It is not a work of self-advertisement. The iconographer avoids stylistic innovations intended to take the place of a signature. This does not preclude the names of certain iconographers being known to us, but we can say that the greater the iconographer, the less he or she seeks personal recognition. Similarly the icon painter does not use iconography to promote an ideology or a personal opinion. The iconographer, having been blessed by the Church to carry on this form of non-verbal theological activity, willingly works under the guidance of church canons, tradition, and the hierarchy.

Yet real iconography is not merely the slavish copying of work done by others. Ouspensky writes:

> Tradition never shackles the creative powers of the iconographer, whose individuality expresses itself in the composition as well as in the color and line. But the personal here is much more subtle than in the other arts and so often escapes superficial observation.... Although icons are sometimes remarkably alike, we never find two absolutely

identical icons, except in cases of deliberate copying in more modern times.[15]

The icon is an act of witness. As Thomas Merton explained to a correspondent belonging to a church which avoided religious imagery of any kind:

> What one "sees" in prayer before an icon is not an external representation of a historical person, but an interior presence in light, which is the glory of the transfigured Christ, the experience of which is transmitted in faith from generation to generation by those who have "seen," from the Apostles on down. . . . So when I say that my Christ is the Christ of the icons, I mean that he is reached not through any scientific study but through direct faith and the mediation of the liturgy, art, worship, prayer, theology of light, etc., that is all bound up with the Russian and Greek tradition.[16]

Finally, the icon is a revelation of transfiguration. We were made in the image and likeness of God, but the image has been damaged and the likeness lost. Since Adam and Eve, only in Jesus Christ were these attributes fully intact. The icon shows the recovery of wholeness. Over centuries of development, iconographers gradually developed a way of communicating physical reality illuminated by the hidden spiritual life. The icon suggests the transfiguration that occurs in whoever, as the Orthodox say, has "acquired the Holy Spirit." The icon is thus a witness to *theosis:* deification. "God became human so that the human being could become God."

The Making of an Icon

The first iconographer I ever met was Father Zinon, a young monk of the Monastery of the Caves near Pskov, not far from the Russian border with Estonia. I was there on a bright winter day early in 1987. I had wanted to meet him since learning he had painted the iconostasis of the Church of the Protecting Veil at the Danilov Monastery in Moscow. I knew people who compared Father Zinon's work with the icons of Rublev.

The monastery is built into a deep fold between densely wooded hills. Nearly a mile of thick fortress walls are wrapped around this thicket of churches and other colorful buildings: gold, ultramarine, magenta, lemon, crimson, moss green, turquoise, and snow white. Monks have lived here since 1400. Despite invasions, occupations, revolutions, and atheist rulers, it has remained a place of uninterrupted prayer. "It is Russia in miniature," said Father Constantine, the priest from Pskov who brought me there.

I had heard from friends about the remarkable hospitality of the people living in the village adjacent to the monastery. "There are no hotels nearby but it doesn't matter," I was told. "There is no need for a hotel. All you have to do is knock on any door in the village. When the door opens, simply say, '*Gospodi pomilui* [Lord have mercy],' and you will be the guest of that family."

"The understanding of God is the understanding of beauty," said Father Nathaniel, the elderly monk who welcomed us. "Beauty is at the heart of our monastic life. The life of prayer is a constant well of beauty. We have the beauty of music in the Holy Liturgy. The great beauty of monastic life is communal life in Christ. Living together in love, living without enmity, as peaceful with each other as one dead body is peaceful with another dead body. We are dead to enmity." I was reminded of Dostoevsky's words in *The Idiot*, "Beauty will save the world."

17

Father Zinon, icon painter and monk.

After venerating the bodies of the saints buried in the caves from which the monastery takes its name, we walked through the snow to Father Zinon's log cabin.

The cabin was newly built and had a large window providing plenty of light. The room itself was warm not only from the stove but from the colors and the smell of paint. In one corner I noticed lapis lazuli stones being soaked in preparation for grinding. All the colors used by the iconographer, Father Zinon explained, come from natural substances, mostly minerals. On the easel was a part of the iconostasis he was painting for another church then under restoration at the Danilov Monastery, the Church of the Seven Ecumenical Councils.

I asked Father Zinon if he had grown up as a believer. "No, though my mother is a believer. I started to come to belief when I was an art student. I was searching for some time for a copy of the Gospels and finally found a copy and then read them through. Then I decided." Though only thirty-three, he already had the directness one associates with the monastic life.

I mentioned several ancient icons that I had admired in the Tretyakov Gallery in Moscow. "They should all be put back in the churches they were taken from," Father Zinon replied. "They are not civil paintings. They aren't for museums. They aren't decorations. They are a reflection that God became man. They are holy doors."

I asked if he felt free to make changes in the traditional images. "Icons carry the real feeling and teaching of Orthodoxy. The icon painter hasn't the right to change an icon just to be different. He is simply the co-author, part of a collective endeavor. It isn't the painter's own work. It is from heaven. We who are called to paint them are not icon producers. We never sign what we paint."

I asked about the iconographer's preparation for painting an icon. "To make an icon is the fulfillment of prayer," Father Zinon responded. "You need to feel the Holy Spirit. You can feel icons only during prayer. And icons are only for prayer. An icon is a place of prayer. You paint it in the same way you prepare for a church service, with prayer and fasting. It is a liturgical work. Preparing to paint an icon is like preparing to celebrate the Holy Liturgy."

In those days I knew practically nothing about how an icon is made. I had my first glimpse of this in Father Zinon's log cabin. Little by little I have come to learn the basics of the craft.

Icons can be made in a variety of media, including mosaic, fresco, and bas-relief, but the main medium is egg tempera on wood. Fundamentals of the method, handed down from generation to generation, predate Christianity.[17]

The icon requires a dry, well-aged, knot-free, non-resinous wood, for example, lime, alder, birch, or cypress, or pine with little resinous content. Two horizontal wedges of a hard wood are often inserted in the back of the panel to counteract warping. Frequently a recessed area is made in the panel, the margins serving both as a frame and protection for the image.

The surface of the wood panel is lightly scored so that it can better hold the material that will be attached to it, as the icon is painted not directly on the wood but on an intermediate surface. Often a piece of loosely woven linen or cheesecloth is glued on, or the board is just "sized" with a mixture of gelatine and hot water with a small amount of chalk or alabaster whiting added. This provides a base for what will follow — the careful application of five to seven thin layers of gesso without air bubbles or any other irregularity or contamination. Each layer must dry slowly for at least twelve hours before the next layer is applied. The process of simply preparing the surface takes at least a week.

When the surface has been very lightly sandpapered and worked over with a smooth flat stone, it will have a silky texture, be slightly matte, and be free from chalk dust.

The outlines of the iconographer's preliminary drawing are then put on tracing paper, after which the back is rubbed with red ocher powder or something similar, at which point the traced lines are gone over again, transferring the outline to the icon's prepared surface.

Next comes the painstaking application of gold leaf to those areas of the icon requiring it — halos and sometimes the entire background area.[18]

Finally the actual painting with egg tempera begins. Fresh

yolk is mixed with water and a small amount of vinegar. Just as effective in reducing the greasiness of the egg yolk is old beer or wine. Sometimes oil of cloves is added as a preservative. This is mixed as needed with pigment ground from minerals or other natural sources, with artificial colors used, if at all, only as supplements. Ouspensky observes:

> When properly mixed these paints are a precious and very convenient material for painting . . . suitable both for brush-work and for the laying on of washes, and a combination of both methods may be varied indefinitely. They dry as rapidly as water colors, but they are not so easily washed off. Their durability increases with time and their resistance to chemical decomposition under the influence of sunlight is much greater than with water colors or oil paints.[19]

In contrast to methods taught in art schools, the painting is built up from a dark base to lighter colors, creating in the process a barely perceptible relief. Finally the outlines are redrawn, highlights added (bright touches, most often in white or liquid gold), and the appropriate inscriptions inserted to identify the figures.

Several weeks later, after the icon has thoroughly dried, it is covered with olifa, a varnish made from boiled linseed oil to which one or more resins, for example, amber, are added. The olifa, permeating the paint down to the wood, both protects the surface of the icon and gives it brightness, depth, and translucency.

Painting an icon not only involves mastering the necessary techniques, possible only through apprenticeship, but is a work of prayer. Making an icon is a work of prayer, fasting, and meditation.

Even when the image is completed, there remains one more essential step: the blessing of the icon. It is kept on the altar table in the sanctuary from Vespers until after the Liturgy the following day and is formally blessed by a priest, ideally in the presence of the owner.

While courses in icon painting are more and more available, the iconographer should really be a person who has been blessed to carry on such work and be recognized as possessing not only the technical ability but the necessary virtues. Six hundred years ago, the Russian Church's Council of One Hundred Chapters ruled that the iconographer must be "meek, mild, pious, not given to idle talk or to laughter, not quarrelsome or envious, not a thief or a murderer."[20]

Prayers of an Iconographer

O Divine Lord of all that exists, You have illumined the Apostle and Evangelist Luke with your Holy Spirit, enabling him to represent your most Holy Mother who held You in her arms and said: "The grace of Him who has been born of me is spread throughout the world." Enlighten and direct my soul, my heart and my spirit. Guide the hands of your unworthy servant so that I may worthily and perfectly portray your image, that of your Mother and all the saints, for the glory, joy, and adornment of your Holy Church. Forgive my sins and the sins of those who venerate this icon and who, praying devoutly before it, give homage to those represented. Protect them from all evil and instruct them with good counsel. This I ask through the intercession of your most Holy Mother, the Apostle Luke, and all the saints. Amen.

O heavenly Master, fervent architect of all creation, light the gaze of your servant, guard his heart and guide his hand, so that worthily and with perfection he may represent your image, for the glory and beauty of your Holy Church. In the name of the Father, Son, and Holy Spirit, now and forever and unto ages of ages. Amen.

Rules for the Icon Painter _____

1. Before starting work, make the sign of the cross; pray in silence, and pardon your enemies.

2. Work with care on every detail of your icon, as if you were working in front of the Lord Himself.

3. During work, pray in order to strengthen yourself physically and spiritually; avoid, above all, useless words, and keep silence.

4. Pray in particular to the saint whose face you are painting. Keep your mind from distractions and the saint will be close to you.

5. When you have to choose a color, stretch out your hand interiorly to the Lord and ask His counsel.

6. Do not be jealous of your neighbor's work; his success is your success too.

7. When your icon is finished, thank God that His mercy has granted you the grace to paint the holy images.

8. Have your icon blessed by putting it on the altar. Be the first to pray before it, before giving it to others.

9. Never forget: the joy of spreading icons in the world, the joy of the work of icon-painting, the joy of giving the saint the possibility to shine through his icon, the joy of being in union with the saint whose face you are painting.[21]

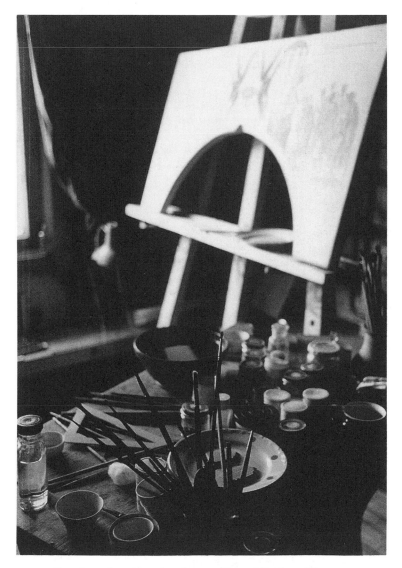

Easel and paints in the studio of Father Zinon.

Color in Iconography

To a great extent the colors used depend on the iconographer, local tradition, and what is available. As you study different versions of any icon, you will find dramatic differences in color choices, though each must be suitable to the theological meaning of the icon. Some general comments:

- Blues are associated with heaven, mystery, and the mystical life. Dark blue is often used in the cloak Christ wears in the Pantocrator icon as well as the clothing of Mary, the Mother of God.

- Green signifies the earth's vegetation, fertility in a general sense, youth, and freshness. It often is used in the clothing of martyrs, whose blood nurtures the Church.

- Brown is linked with earth and inert matter. In clothing it may be a sign of a life of holy poverty.

- Red, the color of blood, suggests life, vitality, and beauty (in Slavonic the word for beauty and red is the same). The inner robe Christ wears in the Pantocrator icon is red. Orange-red, associated with fire, suggests fervor and spiritual purification.

- Purple is associated with wealth and power.

- White is associated with the divine world, purity, innocence, and is sometimes used with what Orthodoxy calls "the uncreated light," the light that Jesus revealed in the Transfiguration to Peter, James, and John.

- Gold is linked with sanctity, splendor, the imperishable, the divine energy, the glory of God, and life in the kingdom of God.

Part II

Prayer

‡

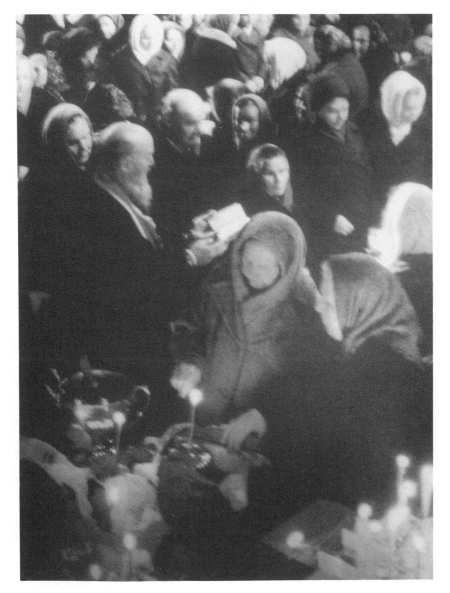

Worshippers in the Orthodox cathedral in Odessa.

The Need to Pray

I am astonished that people are not astonished.

— G. K. CHESTERTON

To pray is to pay attention to something or someone other than oneself. Whenever a man so concentrates his attention... that he completely forgets his own ego and desires, he is praying.[22]

— W. H. AUDEN

In an era of de-mystification, in which everything can be knowingly explained in such a way that it becomes as flat and dull as old wallpaper, prayer can seem an absurd activity, something for the simple-minded. We stand before God reciting lines from an ancient play, not sure we believe what we are saying or even that the God whom we address exists, or that the saints we invoke are anything more than faded memories. Even for those blessed by strong belief, coming before God in prayer can overwhelm them with a sense of their own ridiculousness. Prayer is an act of simplicity in a complex world, yet in attempting to pray we may discover how far from simplicity we are.

"Only those who are guileless can really pray, for when we pray we can deceive no one, not the Mother of God, not the saints, not God Himself, not even ourselves," my friend Mark Pearson remarked in a recent letter. "So we are left naked, bereft, in the starkness of our attempt to come into the presence of the Almighty. We feel inadequate, unworthy, our feeble attempts at prayer seem so pathetic, futile even. Yet in just making the effort to pray, it seems that we achieve something, however minuscule. But it is hard. We feel vulnerable and somehow embarrassed, especially in front of other people. I am a parent of young children, and for many parents, prayer is more difficult to handle than nudity. We see nudity as natural for young children, but we expect that they will grow out of it. So it is with prayer. Prayer is natural for young children and it has taken me some time to feel comfortable with both praying together with my children and allowing them to watch me while I am praying, and inviting them to join. How can parents be natural in prayer with their children if we do not pray naturally ourselves?"

We are meant to pray. Prayer is as much a part of being alive as breathing. I can hold my breath only for so long before I *have* to take another breath. If anyone has committed suicide by refusing to breathe, it's news to me. Similarly I wonder if even the most hardened atheist ever gets to the point of being totally incapable of prayer. To the extent a person stops praying, something at the heart of human identity is dying in that individual.

Prayer is among the most persistent and universal of human activities. We know of no culture at any level of development in which some form of prayer doesn't occur. However deeply we dig into the human past, we find traces of spiritual life.

Yet we live in a secular age that tends to regard prayer as having a decorative social function — possibly comforting for some, but non-essential. Secularism, Father Alexander Schmemann realized, is the negation of the human being as *homo adorans,* the being for whom worship is the most essential action, that which makes us truly human.[23] It is our God-given nature to pray, but in a secular society, those who pray may have to endure being thought of as odd.

All that Christians believe and do has its roots in worship. It is through the events of a worshiping life that we experience the sacramentality of all created things. At the same time we discover our neighbors and ourselves as made in God's image, however hidden that image may be. We realize that the world and all our activities in it are means of worship.

Prayer life is in part a consequence of awe. The person who is not amazed is out of touch with reality. To be alive, to be sensitive to beauty, to glimpse the vastness of the cosmos, to become more aware of the hidden structures of being, to watch dancers or skaters, to see people in love, to witness a child learning to walk or speak, to contemplate the faces of other people, to smell freshly baked bread, to watch leaves bursting into the spring air from a barren branch — these and countless ordinary events in life never lose their capacity to astonish. A healthy soul is constantly returning to a condition of wonder. Awe is itself a state of prayer.

Prayer life has to do with being vulnerable and knowing our need for God's help. No matter how much we do to safeguard our lives or to protect ourselves from pain and loss, we aren't safe and we can't escape suffering. It is natural to cry out for help even if we are uncertain there is a Creator listening. It is in these prayers that we admit our needs, and the needs of people we are concerned about, to God.

"You have made us for yourself, O Lord, and our hearts are restless until they rest in you," wrote St. Augustine. At its deepest level, prayer has to do with the longing to be in union with God, to live in the reality of God. There is an underlying loneliness experienced by every human being that can only briefly be displaced by activities, no matter how engaging, or by relationships with people, no matter how much they love each other, no matter how enduring their love, no matter how much they have in common. I sometimes wonder if the wasteful and destructive things people do aren't a way of trying to avoid a God-centered life? But it never works. Probably even Hitler was troubled by God.

Prayer is a word we have for all that we do in our efforts to be in touch with God, or our ways of exploring God, coming to know through actual experience who God is. This is mystical life. To see it from another angle, our spiritual life is a process of doing all we can to rid ourselves of those things in our lives — ideas, ideologies, vices, obsessions — which get in the way of awareness of God.

To the extent we know God, we are drawn to expressions of praise and gratitude. At our most blessed moments, what moves us to pray is not a sense of duty but is similar to what happens to people in love. They can hardly stop thinking about how wonderful the other person is. We pray out of our joy in who God is. "Joy is the most infallible sign of the presence of God," noted the French poet Leon Bloy.

Prayer can also be a response to sorrow and grief. "Blessed are they who mourn" is the second beatitude — the beatitude of tears. To the extent we care about other people, we participate in their losses and suffering. We see the terrible things that happen, also what we have done or failed to do, and realize that truly we are sinners whose situation is hopeless unless God is merciful. Prayer is a cry of the heart for God's mercy.

Yet if we wait to be in the mood to pray, we soon find we haven't much of a prayer life. Prayer is not only for moments when we are deeply moved and words of praise or urgent petition arise spontaneously. Spiritual life gets nowhere without discipline and endurance, a "rule of prayer" that helps shape each and every day. If you want to make headway in prayer, you pray when you are not in the mood, pray when there is no time, pray even if you have no sense of the presence of God. Prayer is like love of your children — you take care of them and their basic needs no matter how you happen to be feeling at that moment. You slowly build up islands of prayer at the beginning and end of each day until prayer is one of the main structures of life.

I know a young man in England who has to drive into London every weekday and is often stuck in traffic jams. "I do my morning prayers when the car isn't moving," he tells me. "By the time I get to work, I've done a good bit of praying!" One of the readers of this book when it was still in draft noted that she prays while riding in the New York City subway while coming and going to work each day at her law office. "But I have to memorize all my prayers," she noted, "because sometimes people harass you if they see a prayer book in your hands."

A problem confronting many people in their struggle to pray is not only a lack of discipline but a faulty conception of God which makes a relationship in prayer inconceivable or unnecessary. One often finds people who see God not so much as someone but as something — a principle of being, as impersonal as gravity, as remote as another galaxy. Others have formed an image of God as the great punisher, an everlasting Stalin. (In describing his grandfather at prayer, Gorky recalls that cranky and miserly old man's main interest as he stood in his icon corner was to remind God who was in need of divine wrath and to give God guidance about the forms that wrath might take.) Still others reduce God to a fountain of automatic forgiveness: their God is so merciful that there is no need to seek mercy.

A problem blocking the way for many people is the idea that the spiritual life is something each person does entirely on his own — in such a view, the Church is not needed and may even be an obstacle. Many people present "institutional Christianity" as something the truly "spiritual person" should avoid like the plague. I would be the first to agree that churches have plenty of faults and contain many difficult people, but there isn't a single social structure, large or small, in which we don't quickly encounter the same problem. In fact the biggest obstacle of all isn't our neighbor but ourselves. Truly, we are our own worst enemies.

If the same anti-social principle were applied to any other area of life, we would soon die of the resulting radical solitude. Few of us grow the food we eat, and none of us invented the basic skills on which our lives depend. We communicate with words not of our own making but handed down to us. We do our work using tools others perfected. We exist because our mothers gave birth to us. The books we read and the films we see were made by others. There is no creature on earth more socially dependent than a human being.

Perhaps we can speak of the church, lower case "c," in a sociological sense, meaning the human reality of the church with all its glaring imperfections, and the Church, upper case "C," meaning Christ's body. In the latter sense, the Church is the divinely founded organism which offers us not only the Bible but the wisdom to understand it, and not only sacred texts but the sacraments. (Still, the problem of finding one's home in Christianity sometimes involves a long and difficult search.)

A common obstacle to prayer is distraction. "I throw myself down in my chamber," the poet and Anglican priest John Donne confessed, "and I call in, and invite God, and his Angels thither, and when they are there, I neglect God and his Angels, for the noise of a fly, for the rattling of a coach, for the whining of a door."[24] Attention to an icon can sometimes help overcome distraction.

Being honest in prayer is another problem for many people. There is a temptation to present ourselves in prayer in our polite "Sunday best," as if God were a sour-tempered great-aunt

Icon corner in the home of a priest near Pskov.

whose main interest was the correct arrangement of silverware and using the right paper for thank you notes. There is no point in putting ourselves on our best behavior when we pray, pretending to be some other, better, more refined person. "We often want one thing and pray for another, not telling the truth even to the gods," observed the Roman writer Seneca two generations before the birth of Christ. For us it might be, "I am one thing and in prayer pretend to be another, not being truthful about who I am even with God."

Most of us live in fear-driven societies, and it is a fact that fear impedes spiritual life. I don't mean the fear of God. Paradoxically, the fear of God puts all other fears in their place. The fear of God is nothing like all those fears which undermine our being. It means to stand in awe of the incomprehensible, the Creator of the universe with all its wonders and mysteries, God who is both more intimate than breath and as remote as the darkness beyond the furthest star. But a person overwhelmed with anxiety tends to limit prayer to complaints and appeals. Keep in mind the advice that angels give in nearly every biblical account we have about them: "Be not afraid." A vital prayer life opens the door for God gradually to help us move fear from the center to the edge of daily life.

Another obstacle to prayer is preoccupation with time.

I remember an experience I had during the late sixties when I was accompanying Thich Nhat Hanh, a Buddhist monk and poet from Vietnam who was giving lectures in the United States. We were at the University of Michigan, waiting for the elevator doors to open. I noticed my brown-robed companion was looking at the electric clock above the elevator doors. Then he said, "You know, Jim, a few hundred years ago it would not have been a clock; it would have been a crucifix."

He was right. The clock is a religious object in our world, one so powerful that it can depose another.

I also recall a story related in his journal by Daniel Wheeler, a Quaker engineer who had gone from Britain to Russia at the time of Tsar Alexander I to take charge of draining swampland in the Ochta region south of St. Petersburg. A group of peasants was sent to his house with an urgent message, knocked on the door, got no response, and went inside to look for the engineer. First things first, however. Once inside, one's first duty as an Orthodox Christian is to find the icon corner and say a few prayers, but this proved difficult. Nothing looked like an icon. The peasants knew things were different in other countries. What would a British icon look like? What impressed them most was the mantelpiece clock. They decided this was a British icon and so crossed themselves, bowed before the clock, and recited their prayers.[25]

In a way the peasants were right. They had identified a machine which has immense power in the lives of "advanced" people.

I think too of an experiment in the sixties at a theological school in America. A number of students were asked to prepare sermons on the Parable of the Good Samaritan. These weren't to be publicly delivered but recorded on tape for grading by a professor of homiletics. It seemed an ordinary assignment, but those responsible for the project were interested in more than what the aspiring pastors would say about the parable. Without their knowledge, the students had been divided into three groups. Some were to be called on a certain morning and told that they could come to the taping room any time in the day; others were to be told that they had to be there within the next few hours; and the rest were to be told that they had to come without delay.

The testers had arranged that, as each student arrived at the building where the sermons were being recorded, they would find someone lying on the ground by a bench near the entrance, seemingly unconscious and in need.

What were the results? Among all those preaching sermons on the Parable of the Good Samaritan, barely a third took the time to stop and do anything for the person lying on the ground. Those who did stop, it was discovered, were mainly the ones who had been told they could come any time that day. They felt they had time, and that *sense of having time* gave them time to be merciful. They weren't overwhelmed with deadlines and overcrowded schedules — the constant problem of many people, not least clergy and lawyers, which perhaps is why Jesus cast a priest and Levite in those unfortunate parts in his parable.

In reality everyone has time, but people walking side by side on the same street can have a very different *sense* of time, so that one of them is so preoccupied by worry or fear or plans for the future that he hardly notices what is immediately at hand, while the next person is very attentive. Each person has freedom — to pause, to listen, to pray, to change direction. Learning to pray in an unhurried way can help us become less hurried people.

It can be hard work learning how to get off the speedway inside our heads. Metropolitan Anthony, the Russian Orthodox bishop in London, suggests as an exercise sitting down and saying to yourself:

> "I am seated, I am doing nothing, I will be doing nothing for five minutes," and then relax, and continually throughout this time (one or two minutes is the most you will be able to endure to begin with) realize, "I am here in the presence of God, in my own presence and in the presence of all the furniture that is around me, just still, moving nowhere."
>
> There is of course one more thing you must do: you must decide that within these two minutes, five minutes, which you have assigned to learning that the present exists, you will not be pulled out of it by the telephone, by a knock on the door, or by a sudden upsurge of energy that prompts you to do at once what you have left undone for the past ten years.
>
> So you settle down and say, "Here I am," and you are. If you learn to do this at lost moments in your life when you have learned not to fidget inwardly, but to be completely calm and happy, stable and serene, then extend the few minutes to a longer time and then to a little longer still.[26]

There are times not to answer the door, not to answer the phone, not to do undone things, but to rest in silence from everything. The world can wait five minutes. In fact no matter how busy we are, no matter how well organized, no matter how little rest we allow ourselves, we will never do everything that needs to be done. But to do well what we are supposed to do, it is essential to nurture a capacity for inner stillness. Such quiet, deep-down listening is itself prayer.

I recall a conversation about listening in silence one of my daughters had with me when she was four or five years old. She asked, "You know what those little sounds are that you hear when you're all alone?" "What's that, Wendy?" "That's God." "What sounds?" I asked. "You know, those sounds you hear when you're alone."

In Orthodoxy the Liturgy truly orders us to rest from our worries. In the middle of the service, the choir sings the Cherubic Hymn, doing so in such a slow way that it always surprises me to see how short a prayer this actually is:

> Let us who mystically represent the Cherubim, and who sing the thrice-holy hymn to the life-creating Trinity, now lay aside all earthly care.

These last few words are a real challenge. Sometimes I completely fail. It is not only difficult to lay aside all earthly cares but there is something in me that is offended by the idea of letting go of all my concerns, worries, projects, and irritations.

The prophet Elizah is the patron saint of quiet waiting. In the Transfiguration icon, we find Moses on one side of Christ, Elizah on the other. Elizah withdrew to his cave on Mount Carmel, hiding from those who threatened his life. In his refuge, God instructed him to stand on the mountain and wait:

> And behold, the Lord God passed by, and a mighty wind tore at the mountain and broke the rock into pieces before the Lord, but the Lord was not in the wind. And after the wind came an earthquake, but the Lord was not in the earthquake. After the earthquake came a fire, but the Lord was not in the fire. And after the fire came a still, small voice. (1 Kings 19:11–12)

It was in a whisper that Elizah heard God, surely not what he expected. He had to wait through much noise and distraction to get there. Not only for Elizah but for anyone, the silence and waiting that is so much a part of prayer creates the possibility of "hearing" God — not in words or noises but in the sharpening of conscience, insight, and understanding.

"Real silence," Metropolitan Anthony writes, "is something extremely intense, it has density and it is really alive." He recalls a story from the Desert Fathers about one of the saints refusing to preach to a visiting bishop: "No, I won't," said the monk, "because if my silence doesn't speak to him, my words will be useless."[27]

Praying in Body and Soul

We bless you now, O my Christ, word of God, light of light without beginning, bestower of the Spirit. We bless you, threefold light of undivided glory. You have vanquished the darkness and brought forth the light, to create everything in it.[28]

— St. Gregory Nazianzen

Pray simply. Do not expect to find in your heart any remarkable gift of prayer. Consider yourself unworthy of it. Then you will find peace. Use the empty, dry coldness of your prayer as food for your humility.[29]

— St. Makari of Optino

"With my body I thee worship," husband and wife declare to each other in the traditional Anglican wedding service. The words are relevant not only to marital love but to the spiritual life.

Angels are bodiless beings; we are not. God has made us body and soul, and to be whole we must worship God body and soul. Nothing is more central to Christianity than its affirmation of the significance of material reality. One of the most important roles played by icons in Christian history has been to proclaim the physical reality of Jesus Christ, God incarnate. He had, and has, a face. He had, and has, a body. In icons of Mary holding her son, we always see his bare feet, a reminder that he walked on the earth. He was born, lived, died, and rose from the dead, breaking bread with disciples in Emmaus, eating fish with them in Galilee, inviting Thomas to feel the wound in his side. Nearly all the miracles Jesus performed were physical healings. So important is the human body that most of the questions to be asked of us at the Last Judgment have to do with our merciful response to the physical needs of others: "I was hungry and you fed me, I was thirsty and you gave me drink, I was naked and you clothed me, I was homeless and you gave me shelter, I was sick and you cared for me..." (Matt. 25:34–37). It is through protective care for creation, most of all care for each other, that we most clearly manifest our love of God.

One of the odd things that has happened to prayer in much of Western Christianity — in some churches with the Reformation, in others more recently — has been the drastic erosion of the physical dimension of spiritual life. Prayer has become mainly an activity of the head. Many of us have become like birds trying to fly with one wing. Icons can help us grow back the missing wing, the physical aspect of prayer.

Do you pray with your eyes closed? Because icons are physical objects, they serve as invitations to keep our eyes open when we pray. While prayer may often be, in Thomas Merton's words, "like a face-to-face meeting in the dark," cutting a major link with the physical world by closing your eyes is not a precondition of prayer. Icons help solve a very simple problem: If I am to pray with open eyes, what should I be looking at? It doesn't have to be icons, but icons are a good and helpful choice. They serve as bridges to Christ, as links with the saints, as reminders of pivotal events in the history of salvation.

Finding icons can seem daunting if you don't know where to look. In fact, though you may not be aware of it, probably you will find them nearby. Just about any local Orthodox parish is likely to have icon prints for sale. Here too you will find help in contacting an iconographer in the event you want to buy or commission a hand-painted icon. Many religious book shops will have icon prints on sale, some of these already mounted on wood. (In case you find no source locally, a selection of addresses for ordering icon prints by mail is provided below on p. 163.)

Once you begin praying with icons, you may find icons have a way of seeking you out. Maria Hamilton, one of the people who read this book in manuscript, wrote to me,

> When an icon wants to be in your icon corner, it just comes to you. There is nothing you can do about it. I was given a small icon when I was chrismated.[30] Then people just started bringing them to me. I started giving one or

two away now and then, and every time I gave one away, two more came in its place. It is possible, with effort, to control the multiplication of books and recordings, but not icons. I never *buy* icons, because they just *come* to live here.

Maria also noted something a priest once said to her: "Do not go out and buy icons. Go downtown and look at Christ in the faces of the poor." For this very reason, during the Orthodox Liturgy it is not only icons that are censed by the deacon or priest but each person standing in the church. If we are indifferent to the image of God in other people, we won't find that image in icons. One thinks of the advice given to medieval pilgrims: "If you do not travel with Him whom you seek, you will not find Him when you reach your destination."

Once you have an icon, it requires a place. There should be an "icon corner" in the place you live: an area where one or several icons are placed that serves as a regular center of prayer. In our small house no actual corner can serve this purpose. For us the fireplace mantel in the living room has become the usual place where my wife and I pray at the start of the day and before we go to sleep at night, though occasionally we use the icon corner in our bedroom.

If you have only one icon, it should be either an icon of the Savior or Mary holding Christ in her arms. If a hand-painted icon is unavailable, get a print of a classic, well-known icon. It should be one that appeals to you, the test being: Does it help you to pray? In time get an icon of your patron saint and of a local or national saint. Keep in mind that an icon is a prototype of the person represented. The icon exists to help connect you.

Icons can be placed in other areas of your home. If there is an icon near the table where meals are served, you may want to begin and end your meals by standing and facing the icon while reciting a prayer before and after the meal. It is good to have an icon in every bedroom and the kitchen.

Depending on your place or places of work, an icon can be near you throughout the day — on your desk, over the sink, on the dashboard of the car or truck.

When traveling, carry a small icon or an icon card (possibly protected by plastic) in your pocket or purse.

During times of prayer, if not for longer periods, a vigil lamp or candle should be lit in your icon corner. A flame is a metaphor for prayer. Its warm flame both encourages prayer and provides the ideal illumination. Icons are not intended for bright illumination.

Begin and end your prayers with an invocation of the Father, Son, and Holy Spirit, at the same time crossing yourself. With this simple gesture we reconnect ourselves with the community of love that exists within God. The invocation of the Holy Trinity combines a physical action with our words of prayer. In word and act, we remind ourselves we are in the presence of God. There is no need to come from a church tradition in which making the sign of the cross is usual. It was a gesture belonging to the whole Church before the great divisions; its recovery will help bring us closer once again. During times of worship the same gesture can be used whenever the Holy Trinity is invoked and also at the beginning of certain prayers, like the Our Father, or in connection with the word "amen."

The main posture for prayer, especially prayers of praise, worship, and thanksgiving, is standing, a physical attitude that also binds us to the Resurrection. Standing also helps keep you in an alert condition, though if you're used to sitting or kneeling, standing for long periods may take some getting used to. If you have a physical problem that makes standing difficult, use whatever works best, the goal being to be wide awake.

Try praying with your hands extended and palms upward, a gesture both of openness to God's grace and the gift of your hands to God.

There are times in prayer when kneeling is appropriate, especially in prayers of sorrow and repentance or fervent intercession. There are also times to press your forehead against the floor and to lie prostrate.

There are no rules governing postures of prayer. Experiment and be flexible.

Even though you may feel under the pressure of the day and its demands, try not to pray in a hurry. Better to pray for a short time with quiet attention to each word and each indrawn

Easter bread before iconostasis in an Orthodox church in Kiev.

breath than to recite many prayers in a rush. Be aware that we live in a culture in which the clock has become not only a tool of social coordination, but of domination. It can be seen as the principal religious symbol of the secular age.

Be aware of your breathing. You are breathing in life itself, breathing in God's peace. You are breathing out praise and gratitude, breathing out your appeals for help.

If in the midst of prayer a phrase catches your attention or warms your heart, don't rush on with the rest of the prayer but stop to pray again and again these few words.

Cultivate an inner attitude of listening. "In prayer," noted St. Theophan the Recluse, a nineteenth-century Russian bishop who was spiritual father to many people, "the principal thing is to stand before God with the mind in the heart, and to go on standing before Him unceasingly day and night until the end of life." This is the practice of the presence of God — nurturing a moment-to-moment consciousness of God's intimate closeness. Note St. Theophan's stress on the heart: "Stand before God with the mind in the heart." Prayer is love-centered. It is not so much belief in God that matters but love of God, and similarly love of others, even love of enemies.

God is not an idea and praying is not an exercise to improve our idea of God, though for those of us who have spent a good deal of our lives in classrooms, it can be difficult to get beyond the world of ideas. Prayer is the cultivation of the awareness of God's actual presence. Consider these words of Thomas Merton to his fellow monks at the Abbey of Gethsemani just a few years before his death:

> Life is this simple: We are living in a world that is absolutely transparent and God is shining through it all the time. This is not just a fable or a nice story. It is true. If we abandon ourselves to God and forget ourselves, we see it sometimes, and we see it maybe frequently. God manifests Himself everywhere, in everything, in people and in things and in nature and in events. It becomes very obvious that He is everywhere and in everything and we cannot be without Him. You cannot be without God. It's impossible. It's simply impossible.[31]

There are various ways to pray.

One way is the use of traditional prayers which gradually you come to know by heart. You probably already have one or more books with services of morning and evening prayer; in the back of this book there is a selection of prayers from the Orthodox tradition. Standing in your icon corner or wherever you happen to be praying, use these services or parts of them as time allows.

Don't be distressed that you are using borrowed words. They gradually become your own. When you say them attentively, they become vehicles for things you might never find words for. Reciting words becomes in the end a way of silence and listening. The words have been given to us by the Church and their repetition helps push away distractions and brings us into a state of deeper awareness of God. Because the words are usually ancient, there is a sense in which we are praying in eternity.

There are small prayers that can be said again and again. The Jesus Prayer is the most important of these:

> Lord Jesus Christ, Son of God,
> have mercy on me, a sinner.

It can also be said in shorter variations: "Lord Jesus, have mercy on me," or just, "Jesus, mercy." Sometimes, when thinking about events such as war or catastrophe, it isn't enough to pray only for yourself. Then the prayer may become, "Lord Jesus Christ, Son of God, have mercy on us." The Jesus Prayer, also known as the Prayer of the Heart, helps draw one more and more deeply into the mercy of Christ. It can become so much a part of life that you find yourself praying while walking, waiting in line, or stuck in a traffic jam, struggling with anger or depression, or lying awake in bed unable to go back to sleep. The prayer can be linked to your breathing.[32]

There are also short prayers to Mary. Roman Catholics using the rosary will know the Hail Mary:

Hail Mary, full of grace, the Lord is with thee. Blessed art thou among women and blessed is the fruit of thy womb,

Jesus. Holy Mary, Mother of God, pray for us sinners now and at the hour of our death.[33]

There is the prayer of pouring out your heart to God, as you saw a grandmother doing in the account by Gorky used in the introduction to this book. Try to let the main part of such spontaneous prayer center on praise and thanksgiving, but if you are worried or frightened, angry or in urgent need, express it freely and ask for God's help. Your words can either be spoken aloud or said silently. Don't worry that what you say may come with difficulty and awkwardness.

Pray daily for others. Keep a list of people in need of prayer. Be sure to include not only those you love but anyone you regard as an adversary or enemy. If the list of names gets to be too long for one day, spread it over several days. Keep a prayer list not only for the living but for the dead. Here is an Orthodox prayer you may find useful:

> O God of spirits and of all flesh, who has trampled down death, overthrown the devil and given life to the world, give rest to the souls of thy departed servants [mention their names]. Pardon every transgression which they have committed, voluntary or involuntary, whether by word, deed, or thought. Establish them where the just repose: a place of brightness, a place of refreshment, a place of rest, where all sickness, sighing, and sorrow have fled away.

There is the prayer of simply standing in silence, waiting before the Lord. Such prayer can come at times of joy or grief or exhaustion, when words seem dead or useless or you feel as dry and empty as a desert. Icons can easily draw you into a silence that overwhelms all surrounding noise and distractions.

It is prayer just to look attentively at an icon and let God speak to you. Though some icons are better than others and reveal more, almost any icon has something to offer. Gradually you will find the icons that you need to find — or, as it sometimes seems, they will find you.

Reading the Bible, reading the Fathers of the Church, reading texts from the saints and lives of the saints — this too can be a form of prayer.

Be strict with yourself in setting aside time for prayer. At the beginning it can be very difficult. For many, prayer in the morning is hardest. Everyone is in a rush — to get to work, to get children up and ready and out the door to school — so that stopping for even a few minutes of prayers seems impossible. But what if you were to get up just fifteen minutes earlier? Even before such a small step can be taken, you have to begin to imagine what a difference it makes to begin the day with prayer.

Similarly make it your rule not to go to bed without having prayed. Again, in the beginning it can be a hard struggle to overcome all the habits that exclude prayer, one of which may be the fear that one or another member of the family regards your efforts to pray as laughable. This is an age in which many people are kept from going far in their spiritual lives simply because they are embarrassed to be seen as religious.[34] I often recall Catholic Worker foundress Dorothy Day's remark: "If I have accomplished anything in my life it was because I wasn't afraid to talk about God." Neither was she afraid to be seen at prayer.

If you wake up in the night and can't get back to sleep, you can pray in bed, or you can get up and go to your icon corner to pray. Read the psalms. Get out your list of people you are worried about and take time to pray for them. Sometimes it is in the small hours of the night that spontaneous prayer comes most easily.

While prayer is most often a solitary activity scattered throughout the day, look for opportunities to pray with others. My wife and I stand before our icons before going to bed. Occasionally we are joined by guests. In the beginning our effort required reading together parts of the service of evening prayer used in the Orthodox Church but gradually the prayers are learned by heart and no book is needed. We end our prayers with intercession. We have come to recognize this part of the day as one of the essential activities of our married life, binding us more and more closely together. (It is partly due to the icon corner that the television set was exiled to another part of the house some years ago.)

Be aware of the impact of food on your spiritual life. In the traditional practice of the Church, now slowly being rediscovered in the West, there are several seasons of fasting that precede the great feasts plus two days each week for fasting during the rest of the year: Wednesday and Friday. Fasting in Orthodox practice normally involves abstaining from meat, dairy products, and anything alcoholic. For those not used to going without these things, even very limited fasting seems daunting at first, but as you get used to it, you will notice the difference it makes in your prayer life. Finally you get to the point where you welcome fast days and look forward to seasons of fasting. (Greek and Russian cookbooks often have helpful sections on food for Lent.) Fasting seasons are linked with increased time for prayer and expanded almsgiving.

If you haven't got one already, get a church calendar so that you can follow not only the major seasons but the religious meaning of each day and the associated biblical readings. The liturgical year is a procession of icons through which we keep returning to the main events of salvation history. The purpose of the church year, wrote Father Lev Gillet, is not only to bring to the mind of believers the teachings of the Gospel and the main events of Christian history in a certain order, or to orient our prayer in a certain direction, but "to renew and in some sense actualize the event of which it is a symbol, taking the event out of the past and making it immediate."[35] Through the calendar, we begin to see each day as having more than a secular identity but as a door toward closer union with Christ.

The church calendar also provides us a guide to readings from the Bible for each day of the year. Read the day's texts not with scholarly detachment but with a real thirst to hear God's voice.

One prayer that you might use at the beginning of each day comes from the Monastery of Optino, an important center of spiritual life in Russia in the nineteenth century:

Lord, grant that I may meet the coming day with spiritual tranquility. Grant that in all things I may rely upon your holy will. In each hour of the day, reveal your will to me. Whatever news may reach me this day, teach me to accept it with a calm soul, knowing that all is subject to your holy will. Direct my thoughts and feelings in all my words and actions. In all unexpected occurrences, do not let me forget that all is sent down by you. Grant that I may deal firmly and wisely with every member of my family and all who are in my care, neither embarrassing nor saddening anyone. Give me the strength to bear the fatigue of the coming day with all that it shall bring. Direct my will and teach me to pray, to believe, to hope, to be patient, to forgive, and to love. Amen.

Part III

The Face of the Savior
and
Icons of the Great Feasts

☦

Portion of the iconostasis at the Danilov Monastery, Moscow
(painted by Father Zinon).

Christ, Pantocrator:
Lord of Creation _____

Christianity is the revelation not only of the Word of God, but also of the Image of God, in which His likeness is revealed.[36]
— LEONID OUSPENSKY

When we see friends or relatives after a time apart, we not only tell what has happened since our last meeting but we enjoy sharing visual information. We carry with us family photos. At home and work there are likely to be places where we have similar photos. Many people are avid keepers of photo albums. Perhaps the prehistoric cave paintings at Lascaux in France and similar places have to do with the same aspect of being human. We are the only creatures that make visual records of the things that matter to us.

One way of describing the Church is to say that it is a community of memory. Eucharistic experience connects us with Christ in the most intimate way. In consecrating the bread and wine at the altar, the priest repeats the words, "Do this in memory of me."

Don't think that the Church remembers only the words of the Savior and that the only repository of apostolic memory is the text in the New Testament. Some of those who saw his face painted it.

By the time Jesus was born, the visual arts had reached a high level. Portraiture in the Greek, Roman, and Egyptian civilizations often achieved almost photographic realism. It isn't surprising that Eusebius had seen portraits of Christ dating from apostolic times.

It may even be that one of the icons, "The Savior Not Made by Human Hands," is copied from a miraculous image of his face that Christ imprinted on a linen cloth. Whether this is pious legend or a fact of history one can argue, but what need

not be doubted is the painstaking effort of the first generation of Christians to pass on to succeeding generations, in both
word and image, what they had witnessed, including their vivid
memory of the face of Jesus Christ. Thus century after century
one finds an amazing continuity in icons of Jesus. Similarly one
can easily recognize Mary and the Apostles Peter and Paul.

The iconographer is a bearer of the Church's memory and
experience, known to many people in every generation, of who
Jesus Christ is — a man who walked the roads of Galilee and
Judea and at the same time is Lord of Creation, King of Glory,
Ruler of All. Such phrases can serve to translate the Greek word
Pantocrator.

In the Pantocrator icon we see the face of Jesus Christ, but
we see more than could be photographed had a camera existed
two thousand years ago. It reveals who he really is. We are face
to face with the Jesus Christ, Son of God, Savior, God incarnate,
whose touch or word heals the blind, raises the dead, and drives
out demons.

It is the difficult aim of iconography to show Christ simultaneously as true God and true man, the two made whole in his
person. It took many generations of iconographic effort to find
ways to move beyond classical portraiture.

Part of the solution is the large halo containing broad
cross-like lines that are used only in connection with Christ.
Associated with the cross pieces are three Greek letters, ὁ ὣ ν,
representing the words that Moses heard when he stood before the burning bush and God revealed his name: "I am he
who is" or simply, "the Being." Adjacent to the halo we see the
name of the Savior, IC XC, an abbreviation of Jesus Christ. (The
canons of iconography require that the names of the persons
represented appear on every icon.)

Little by little iconographers learned a way of painting which
suggests a light source that is within rather than outside. The
resulting painting technique builds light on darkness rather
than the other way round. There is, as Ouspensky notes,
"a minimum of detail and a maximum of expressiveness."[37]
Christ's austere but beautiful garments, often highlighted in
gold, remind us that he is higher than kings and emperors. The
colors used suggest divinity and power.

Christ's right hand offers a gesture of blessing, for he came into the world not to condemn but to save. Often his fingers also form the letters abbreviating his name, IC XC.

In his left hand he holds the Gospel Book, a reminder that we find him in his words, written by witnesses and guarded by the Church. In some icons the book is closed, in others open to reveal one or another sentence of his teaching. Among texts often used are "I am the way, the truth, and the life" and "I am the light of the world."

Just as with furniture or architectural forms, the Gospel Book is shown in inverse perspective. Since the Renaissance, most of Western painting has created an illusion of three-dimensional space with an imaginary vanishing point far beyond the painting; inverse perspective makes the book seem to enlarge on the side that rests against Christ.

Some versions of the icon show the Savior standing full length or seated on a throne, a metaphor for his cosmic kingship. When the throne is shown, it is upheld by the seraphim, powerful angelic beings the prophet Isaiah described: "Above him stood the seraphim; each had six wings: with two he covered his face, and with two he covered his feet, and with two he flew" (Isa. 6:2). Christ is contained within an oval *mandorla*,[38] a much-used iconographic device symbolizing heaven and the glory of God. The red corners outside the mandorla each contain symbols of one of the four Gospel authors. They are present because the Gospels, like the angelic powers, also uphold Christ, Pantocrator. (*See color section.*)

In some versions of the Pantocrator icon, we find ourselves before a fierce Christ, the Christ who forcibly expelled the money-changers from the Temple and who spoke scathingly of hypocrites who were like vipers and whitewashed tombs, the Christ who condemned those who loaded on others burdens they would not carry themselves. In other versions, there is an awesome sense of Christ's capacity to forgive seventy times seven. In still others we seem to find every word in the Gospels — we are simultaneously conscious both of his healing miracles and his rigorous demands, aware of his infinite mercy and the fact that we will be judged for what we did and what we failed to do. Aspects of Christ which seem irreconcilably opposed when described verbally become seamlessly one in the immense silence of his face.

Looking at this icon, which so often calls me to account, I am sometimes reminded of a story Dostoevsky heard from an old *babushka* and made part of *The Brothers Karamazov*. In it a self-centered woman is almost saved from hell by an onion. "But she wasn't entirely selfish," said her guardian angel, standing before the throne of God. "Remember, she once gave an onion to a hungry beggar." "Yes, that's true," said the Creator, who chose not to remind the angel that the onion had not been so much given as thrown and that it had been a rotten onion. "I bless you to use an onion to lift her out of hell." The angel took the onion and found the stingy woman in her place in hell. She quickly grabbed hold of the onion and was being lifted up, but those standing nearby hung on to her legs so that they could be rescued with her. The woman, still ruled by selfishness, wanted heaven only for herself, so she kicked the others away. "Just for me," she screamed, "just for me!" As she said these words, the onion became so rotten that it could no longer carry her weight and she fell back into hell.

Contemplation of the face of Christ can save us from the hell of our own fear and selfishness.

When distracted during the Liturgy, I find it helpful to gaze at the Pantocrator icon that, in Orthodox churches, is just to the right of the royal doors in the center of the iconostasis. The icon reminds me that I am truly standing before Christ. It helps bring me back to reality, back to the present moment, back to the consciousness that I am always in the presence of God and that each choice I make, each word I speak, every moment of attention or inattention, has significance and has something to do with the person I will be when I am raised from the dead for the Last Judgment: a person in communion — or out of communion.

Annunciation _____

In the days of the creation of the world, when God was uttering his living and mighty "Let there be," the word of the Creator brought creatures into the world. But on that day, unprecedented in the history of the world, when Mary uttered her brief and obedient, "So be it," I hardly dare say what happened then — the word of the creature brought the Creator into the world.[39]

> — METROPOLITAN PHILARET OF MOSCOW,
> a sermon on the Feast of Annunciation, 1874

We know little about Mary before the Annunciation. The Church recalls that her parents were Anne and Joachim, always invoked at the end of the Orthodox Liturgy. No words better communicate how blessed is the vocation of marriage than the icon of Anne and Joachim embracing. Mary grew up in pious and loving surroundings, receiving from her parents and others she knew a longing for the Messiah. She was totally awake, deeply sensitive, and fearless. Her compassion for all who suffered was expressed to her cousin Elizabeth: "He who is mighty has done great things for me and holy is his name. His mercy is on those who fear him from generation to generation. He has shown strength with his arm. He has scattered the proud in the imagination of their hearts. He has put down the mighty from their thrones and exalted them of low degree. He has filled the hungry with good things and the rich he has sent empty away" (Luke 1:46–55). Burning words.

In all versions of the Annunciation icon, Mary is on the right, the Archangel Gabriel on the left, while at the top of the icon is a partially revealed dark sphere, symbol of heaven. In many icons rays of divine power radiate from the sphere toward Mary.

Gabriel (from the Hebrew for "God is mighty") is one of the seven archangels, magnificent ethereal beings who lead the heavenly host. The word "angel" comes from the Greek for messenger. Angels are ready to move instantly in the service of God. Wings, always used in iconography to identify angels, suggest their readiness to go wherever God sends them. Though normally invisible to our eyes, angels can, when needed, make themselves visible. Rays of light are often used in highlighting angelic robes to suggest their immaterial existence. "Angels [are] bearers of Divine Silence," writes St. Dionysius the Areopagite, "lights of revelation sent by the inaccessible to reveal him on the very threshold of his sanctuary."[40]

Gabriel's greeting to Mary has been a rich source of meditation throughout the history of Christianity: "Hail, you who are filled with grace, the Lord is with you" (Luke 1:28). The angel's raised right hand signifies the words. Gabriel continues, "Do not be afraid, Mary, for you have found favor with God. Behold, you will conceive in your womb and bear a son, and you shall call him Jesus." Bewildered, Mary asks, "How can this happen, as I have no husband?" Gabriel replies, "The Holy Spirit will come over you and the power of the Most High will overshadow you. Therefore the child to be born will be called holy, the Son of God."

Because Mary became the meeting place of heaven and earth, in Orthodox churches the Annunciation icon is placed on the royal doors directly in front of the altar, the main entrance to the sanctuary — the sanctuary representing, in the symbolism of church architecture, the kingdom of God. Before the royal doors, each baptized person receives the body and blood of Christ. With the Annunciation, Mary received God, body and soul. In receiving communion, we do the same.

A large twelfth-century icon of the Annunciation, now hanging in Moscow's Tretyakov Gallery, was once part of the iconostasis of the convent church at Ustyug near Novgorod.[41] This masterpiece contains no architectural detail or furnishing. At the top, in the heavenly sphere, we see a small representation of Christ enthroned in heaven. Below, Gabriel stands reverently before Mary while she, with inclined head and an expression of loving submission and deep calm, looks outward. In her left hand is a womb-like skein of blood-red thread, a strand of which falls away, then rises to her right hand, dropping away on the other side: a line across her body symbolizing the conception of Christ caused by the Holy Spirit. She wears a dark red shawl. Of a similar color and thus hardly visible, we discover the child enthroned within her, God's hidden presence, an image similar to the Mother of God of the Sign. The fingers of her right hand nearly touch the tiny figure—Christ, who has leapt into human flesh. (*See color section.*)

In other versions of the icon, Gabriel seems to be bounding in while Mary is seated. In these we sense Mary's surprise, even fright, in the first moments of her encounter with the angel. In still others, we see her at the moment when she has moved beyond fear and has offered her world-renewing response, "I am the servant of the Lord. Let it happen as you have said."

Two buildings in the background are linked by a red cloth, a symbol of the reconnection of a divided cosmos made possible by the Incarnation.

My wife tells me that the icon reminds her of the struggle to give up control that each woman faces in giving birth. For everyone, man or woman, it is an image of letting go of the tenacious grip of plans, ideologies, attachments, peer group pressure—all those things which become barriers between ourselves and God. The joy of the Annunciation is not the joy of success or rewards or social prestige but the joy of living in the freedom of God.

Christs Nativity _____

What shall we offer you, O Christ, who for our sake has appeared on earth as man? Every creature made by you offers you thanks. The angels offer you a hymn; the heavens, a star; the Magi, gifts; the shepherds, their wonder; the earth, its cave; the wilderness, the manger; and we offer you a virgin mother.[42]

— FROM A PRAYER FOR THE ORTHODOX
CHRISTMAS VESPERS SERVICE

In a culture in which a sense of the presence of God is increasingly rare, many people see Christ as a long-dead, myth-shrouded teacher who lives on only in fading memory. There are scholars busily at work trying to find out which words attributed to Jesus in the New Testament were actually said by him. Yet even skeptics celebrate Christmas, at least in a limited way. The problem of miracles doesn't intrude, for what could be more usual than birth? If Jesus lived, he was born, and so with little or no faith in the rest of Christian doctrine we can celebrate his birth whatever our degree of faith. Pascha is more and more lost to us, but at least some of the joy of Christmas remains. Perhaps in the end this feast will lead us back to faith in all its richness. We will be rescued by Christmas.

The traditional icon of the Nativity, ancient though it is, takes note of our "modern" problem. There on the lower right we find a despondent Joseph listening to a figure who represents what we might call "the voice of unenlightened reason." As icons are so deeply silent, we are free to wonder about Joseph's morose condition. One explanation is that he cannot quite believe what he has experienced. Divine activity intrudes into our lives in such a mundane, physical way. A woman gives birth to a child as women have been doing since Eve. Joseph has witnessed that birth and there is nothing different about it, unless it be that it occurred in abject circumstances, in a cave in which animals are kept in cold weather. Joseph has had his dreams, he has heard angelic voices, he has been reassured in a variety of ways that the child born of Mary is none other than the Awaited One, the Anointed, God's Son. But still belief comes hard. The labor of giving birth is arduous, as we see in Mary's reclining figure — and so is the labor to believe. Mary has completed this stage of her struggle, but Joseph still grapples with his.

The theme is not only in Joseph's face. The rigorous black of the cave of Christ's birth in the center of the icon represents all human disbelief, all fear, all hopelessness. In the midst of a starless night in the cave of our despair, Christ, "the Sun of Truth," enters history having been clothed in flesh in Mary's body. It is just as the Evangelist John said in the beginning of his Gospel: "The light shines in the darkness and the darkness cannot overcome it."

The Nativity icon is in sharp contrast to the sentimental imagery we are used to in Western Christmas art. In the icon there is no charming Bethlehem bathed in the light of the nativity star but only a rugged mountain with a few plants. The austere mountain suggests a hard, unwelcoming world in which survival is a real battle — the world since our expulsion from Paradise.

The most prominent figure in the icon is Mary, framed by the red blanket she is resting on — the color of life, the color of blood. Orthodox Christians call her the Theotokos: God-bearer, or Mother of God. Her quiet but wholehearted assent to the invitation brought to her by the Archangel Gabriel has led her to Bethlehem, making a cave at the edge of a peasant village the center of the universe. He who was distant has come near, first filling her body, now visible in the flesh.

As is usual in iconography, the main event is moved to the foreground, free of its surroundings. So the cave is placed behind rather than around Mary and her child.

The birth occurs in a cave that was being used as a stable. In fact the cave still exists in Bethlehem. Countless pilgrims have prayed there over the centuries. It no longer looks like a cave. In the fourth century, at Emperor Constantine's order, it was made into a chapel. At the same time, above the cave, a basilica was built.

We see in the icon that Christ's birth is not only for us but for all creation, including voiceless animals. The donkey and the cow stand for "all creatures great and small," endangered, punished, and exploited by human beings. They too are victims of the Fall. Christ's Nativity is for them as well as for us.

There is something about the way Mary turns away from her son that makes us aware of a struggle different from Joseph's struggle. She knows very well her child has no human father, but she does not know her child's future, only that it is clear from the circumstances of his birth that his way of ruling is in absolute contrast to the way kings rule. The ruler of all rules from a manger in a stable. His death on the cross will not surprise her. It is implied in his birth.

We see that the Christ child's body is wrapped "in swaddling clothes." In icons of Christ's burial, you will see he is wearing similar bands of cloth, as does Lazarus in the icon of his raising by Christ. In the Nativity icon, the manger looks much like a coffin. In this way the icon links birth and death. The poet Rilke says we bear our death within us from the moment of birth. The icon of the Nativity says the same. Our life is one piece and its length of much less importance than its purity and truthfulness.

Some versions of the icon show more details, some less.

Normally in the icon we see angels who are worshiping God-become-man. Though we ourselves are rarely aware of the presence of angels, they are deeply enmeshed in our history and we know some of them by name. This momentous event is for them as well as us.

Often the iconographer includes the three wise men who have come from far off, whose close attention to activity in the heavens made them come on pilgrimage in order to pay homage to a king who belongs, not to one people, but to all people, not to one age, but to all ages. They represent the world beyond Judaism.

Then there are the shepherds, the simple people summoned by angels to respond to Christ's birth. Throughout history it has in fact been the simple people who have been most uncompromising in their response to the Gospel, who have not buried God in footnotes. Not the wise men but the shepherds were permitted to hear the choir of angels singing God's praise.

On the bottom right of the icon often there are one or two midwives washing the newborn baby. The detail is based on apocryphal texts concerning Joseph's arrangements for the birth. Those who know the Old Testament will recall the disobedience of midwives to the Egyptian pharaoh; thanks to one of them, Moses was not murdered at birth. In the Nativity icon the midwife's presence has another still more important function, underscoring Christ's full participation in human nature.

Iconographers may leave out or alter various details, but always there is a ray of divine light that connects heaven with the baby. The partially revealed circle at the very top of the icon symbolizes God the Father, the small circle within the descending ray represents the Holy Spirit, while the child is the Second Person of the Holy Trinity, the Son. At every turn, from iconography to liturgical text to the physical gesture of crossing oneself, the Church has always sought to confess God in the Holy Trinity.

The partial circle is also connected with the star that led the magi to the cave. Orthodoxy often speaks of Christ in terms of light and this, too, is suggested by the ray connecting heaven to the manger. "Our Savior, the dayspring from on high, has visited us, and we who were in shadow and in darkness have found the truth," the Church sings on Christmas, the Feast of Christ's Nativity According to the Flesh.

The iconographic portrayal of Christ's birth is not without radical social implications. Christ's birth occurred where it did, we are told by Matthew, "because there was no room in the inn." He who welcomes all is himself unwelcome. From the first moment, he is something like a refugee, as indeed he soon will be in the very strict sense of the word, in Egypt with Mary and Joseph, at a safe distance from the murderous Herod. Later in life he will say to his followers, revealing the criteria of salvation, "I was homeless and you took me in." We are saved not by our achievements but by our participation in the mercy of God — God's hospitality. If we turn our backs on the homeless and those without the necessities of life, we will end up with nothing more than ideas and slogans and be lost in the icon's starless cave.

We return at the end to the two figures at the heart of the icon. Mary, fulfilling Eve's destiny, has given birth to Jesus Christ, a child who is God incarnate, a child in whom each of us finds our true self, a child who is the measure of all things. This is not the Messiah the Jews of those days expected — or the God we Christians of the modern world were expecting either. God, whom we often refer to as all-mighty, reveals himself in poverty and vulnerability. Christmas is a revelation of the self-emptying love of God.

Christs Baptism: Theophany _____

With joy shall you draw water from the wells of Salvation.
— Isaiah 12:3

The Savior is surrounded by water, an iconographic way of representing submersion. His nakedness underscores the theme of self-emptying love shown in many icons of Christ — for the sake of the world and the salvation of the human race, he stripped himself of everything, of every privilege and comfort. Can you recall any paintings of naked kings? Artists went to great lengths to show how richly a ruler was dressed, for opulent clothing revealed wealth and power. In the nakedness of Christ we also see not another emperor but a new Adam.

On the left side of the icon stands the last of the prophets, John the Forerunner, in a garment as rugged as the land surrounding the River Jordan, while on the right three angels worship the Savior. Though stricken with the realization that he is unworthy even to touch the strap of Jesus' sandal, John is baptizing the Messiah. He had begged to exchange places and be himself baptized, but Jesus had insisted that John do to him as he had done to others. "Leave it like this for the present; it is fitting that we should in this way do all that righteousness demands" (Matt. 3:15). The Son of Man had come not to rule but to serve and to take upon himself all the sins of the world. "Being himself the fullness," comments Father Lev Gillet, "he wished to take into himself all that was incomplete and unfinished."[43]

What will become the rite of entrance into the Church, baptism, has its origin in this event in the Jordan. The water is both grave and womb; the old, unredeemed self is drowned and a new self is born, made one with Christ. While Christ himself had no need for baptism, he not only provided a pattern for the sacrament, but in his baptism we see his Crucifixion and Resurrection prefigured.

Icon of the Baptism of the Lord.

Yet the event this icon connects us to is more mysterious than baptism. The word "Theophany" comes from the Greek and means the showing or manifestation of God. What is of primary importance in Christ's baptism is that it was a revelation of the Holy Trinity. For this reason, in the hierarchy of festivals, Theophany is third in importance, after Pascha and Pentecost.

On the banks of the Jordan, John heard the voice of God the Father, "This is my beloved Son," while John saw the Holy Spirit descending like a dove and resting on the head of Christ. It is this mystical event, not John's action, that is the real baptism of Christ.

The Father's presence is represented, as in the Nativity icon, with the circle partially visible at the top of the icon. We find the dove-like Holy Spirit in the smaller circle within the ray of divine energy reaching toward the figure of Christ. (Note that Councils of the Orthodox Church have forbidden representing the Father in a fleshly image. The most an iconographer is allowed to do is suggest the Father through such devices as an empty throne, a hand reaching out from a heavenly cloud, or as an angel, as in the Holy Trinity icon. The image of an elderly man with a white beard, though occasionally found in religious imagery, violates the canons of iconography.[44])

The angels on the right also underscore the Holy Trinity: while three, they are so connected as to be in a state of oneness. The icon reminds us of the three angels who appeared to Abraham and Sarah at the oak of Mamre, the Bible's first vivid hint of the Trinity.

Theophany is also the celebration of the beginning of Christ's public ministry. Few had been called to worship in the stable of his birth, and for three decades afterward almost nothing is known of his activities. In coming to John for baptism, Jesus reveals himself to those whom he is saving.

The Orthodox Church's celebration of the Feast on January 6[45] includes the solemn blessing of water. In Russia I have seen an entire parish troop off in falling snow to do this at the nearest river. After the ice is broken, the priest traces the sign of the cross in the frigid water while the choir sings the hymns of the day:

You have descended into the waters and have given light to all things.... Where indeed should your light have shone except upon those who dwell in darkness?... The nature of water is sanctified.... Let us then draw water in gladness, O brethren, for upon those who draw with faith, the grace of the Spirit is invisibly bestowed by Christ the God and Savior of our souls.

Just as the Son of God became a man of flesh and blood through Mary, he used the material things of our world as means of salvation: water, wine, oil, and bread. The water we bathe in, the water we drink, the water that is the main component of our bodies — every drop of water connects us with the water in which Jesus was baptized.

In Jesus' baptism all water has forever been blessed. In a sense the annual blessing at Theophany is not needed. In blessing what is already blessed, the Church is simply revealing the true nature and destiny of water, and therefore the sacramental nature of all creation. "By being restored through the blessing to its proper function," wrote Father Alexander Schmemann, " 'holy water' is revealed as the true, full, adequate water, and matter becomes again a means of communion with and knowledge of God."[46]

I recall a story I heard over lunch at the Monastery of the Protection of the Mother of God in Kiev. At the request of a Jewish neighbor with an eye disease, a woman had walked to a distant monastery to fetch water from a famous spring associated with miracles. "It was a hot day," said Father Timothy, the monastery's chaplain. "On the way back the woman became so thirsty she drank all the water she was carrying. When she returned home, she filled the empty bottle from the tap and gave this to her sick neighbor. It was just ordinary tap water, but the neighbor's eyes were healed. She had faith that it was holy water."

"You see, all water is holy," said Father Timothy. "All water comes from the River Jordan."

Transfiguration

Just as the Lord's body was glorified when he went up the mountain and was transfigured into the glory of God and into infinite light, so the saints' bodies also are glorified and shine as lightning.[47]

— St. MACARIUS, The Homilies

God became man that we might become God.
— St. IRENAEUS, St. ATHANASIUS, St. GREGORY OF NAZIANZEN, St. GREGORY OF NYSSA, AND OTHER FATHERS OF THE CHURCH

Little by little Jesus revealed himself to his followers, but only three of them were permitted to glimpse the glory of his divinity. Jesus brought Peter, James, and John, his most intimate disciples, to a high place — Mount Tabor in Galilee is the probable location. (In honor of the Transfiguration, St. Helena arranged the construction of a church there in 326.) While praying, the Apostles saw Jesus in conversation with the lawgiver Moses and the prophet Elizah. Christ's clothing became "dazzling white" and his face "shone like the sun."

From Luke's Gospel, we know what Jesus, Moses, and Elizah were discussing: the impending departure of Jesus and what he was to accomplish in Jerusalem.

As Moses and Elizah were leaving, Peter said to Jesus, "Master, it is good that we are here. Let us make three booths, one for you, one for Moses and one for Elizah." Then a radiant cloud overshadowed them. The terrified disciples heard the voice of God the Father saying, "This is my beloved son, my chosen. Listen to him!" (Luke 9:28–36). After the Transfiguration, in Matthew's account, Christ says to the three, "Rise, and have no fear" (Matt. 17:7). Later in life Peter would declare,

For we did not follow cleverly devised myths when we made known to you the power and coming of our Lord Jesus Christ, but we were eye witnesses of his majesty. For

when he received honor and glory from God the Father...
we heard the voice borne from heaven, for we were with
him on the holy mountain. (2 Pet. 1:16–18)

Because he was a witness to the Transfiguration, it is no wonder that light plays such a vital role in Peter's testimony about
the Lord. The prophetic word, he wrote in the same letter, is
like a "shining lamp in a dark place until the day dawns and
the morning star rises in your hearts."

The Transfiguration icon is a stark realization of the story.
We see Christ in white robes on the height of the mountain,
though different iconographers have used different methods
to represent symbolically the uncreated light of divinity or,
as St. John of Damascus expressed it, "the splendor of the
divine nature." The usual iconographic device is a mandorla
surrounding Christ's body with three concentric circles pierced
by knife-sharp rays of gold or white. What actually was seen
could never be painted. Any artistic attempt at photographic
realism would only mask the event. "The light which illumined
the Apostles," Ouspensky observed, "was not something sen-
sible, but on the other hand it is equally false to see in it an
intelligible reality, which could be called 'light' only metaphor-
ically. The divine light is neither material nor spiritual, for it
transcends the order of the created.... [It] has no beginning
and no end."[48] (*See color section.*)

The light that the Apostles experienced on Mount Tabor,
wrote St. Gregory Palamas, one of Christianity's most articulate mystics, "had no beginning and no end. It remained
uncircumscribed and imperceptible to the senses although it
was contemplated by the apostles' eyes.... By a transformation
of their senses, the Lord's disciples passed from the flesh to
the Spirit."[49] Elsewhere St. Gregory notes that "whoever par-
ticipates in the divine energies...in a sense himself becomes
light. He is united to the light and with the light, he sees what
remains hidden to those who do not have grace. He goes beyond the physical senses and everything that is known [by the
human mind]."[50]

The Transfiguration, like Christ's Baptism, is a revelation of
who Christ is, so much more than the prophet or lawgiver the

disciples at first perceived. It is also a revelation of the Holy Trinity. We hear the voice of the Father and see the light of the Holy Spirit and the blinding face of the Son. "Today on Tabor in the manifestation of your light, O Lord," the Orthodox Church sings on August 6, "your light unaltered from the light of the unbegotten Father, we have seen the Father as light, and the Spirit as light, guiding with light the whole creation."

Moses, carrying the tablets of the law, stands on the right, Elizah on the left. They bear witness that Jesus is the Expected One, the fulfillment of the law and the prophets. Also they each had previously experienced the divine presence: Moses in a thick cloud on top of Mount Sinai, Elizah on Mount Carmel, where God spoke to him in a whisper.

Below them are the stricken disciples, Peter, James, and John. Their locations vary in different versions of the icon as do their physical attitudes, but Peter can be recognized with his beard and curly hair, and John from his red robe. Often Peter is kneeling, John thrown backward, and James shielding himself.

The icon is not only about something that once happened on top of Mount Tabor or even about the identity of Christ. It also concerns human destiny, our resurrection and eventual participation in the wholeness of Christ. We will be able to see each other as being made in the image and likeness of God. We too will be transfigured.

Through Christ we become one with God; the Greek word is *theosis;* in English, deification. "God's incarnation opens the way to man's deification," explains Bishop Kallistos of Diokleia. "To be deified is, more specifically, to be 'christified': the divine likeness that we are called to attain is the likeness of Christ. We are intended, said St. Peter, 'to become sharers in the divine nature'" (2 Pet. 1:4).

If you have ever listened to Handel's oratorio, *The Messiah,* you will remember his musical setting of the words of St. Paul: "Behold, I tell you a mystery. We shall not all sleep but we shall all be changed in a moment, in the twinkling of an eye, at the last trumpet.... And the dead shall be raised incorruptible... and this mortal must put on immortality" (1 Cor. 15:51–53).

We can hardly begin to imagine what we will look like to each other, how razor sharp the edges of existence will become, though it occasionally happens in this life that our eyes are briefly opened and we are truly awake, seeing things with an intensity which we tend to describe as blinding — God-given moments of transfiguration. Thomas Merton used to speak of such life-defining flashes as "kisses from God."

The Raising of Lazarus _____

There are few people in the New Testament we know so much about as Lazarus and his sisters Mary and Martha. They were devoted to Jesus and he to them. He was sometimes a guest in their house in the village of Bethany, a short walk to the east of Jerusalem.

At least on one occasion, he was the cause of friction between the sisters. Martha, a hospitable woman busy in the kitchen but annoyed that Mary was listening so avidly to Jesus, scolded him for keeping Mary from her chores. "Lord, do you not care that my sister has left me to serve alone?" "Martha, Martha," Jesus said, "you are anxious and troubled about many things. Only one thing really matters. Mary has chosen the better part and it will not be taken away from her" (Luke 10:38–42).

But when Lazarus died, it was Martha who took the better part. Few stories in the Bible are told with so much detail. The disciples, John wrote, were reluctant that Jesus should return to Judea, even for the sake of Lazarus, because he would be in mortal danger once he reached Jerusalem. But Jesus insisted.

When they arrived at Bethany, Lazarus was already four days in his tomb. It wasn't Mary who went out to meet him as he approached the village, but Martha. Plain spoken person that she was, she immediately expressed her disappointment that he hadn't come sooner. "Lord, if you had been here, my brother would not have died." Jesus answered, "Your brother will rise again." Martha already knew this. "I know that he will rise again in the Resurrection on the last day." Then Jesus provided one of the most important confessions of who he is: "I am the Resurrection and the life. Whoever believes in me, though he die, will live in me, and whoever lives and believes in me shall never die." Then he asked Martha, "Do you believe this?" "Yes, Lord, I believe that you are the Christ, the Son of God, he who is coming into the world."

After this, Martha went to summon her sister, still in the

house. "The Teacher is here and he is calling for you." Mary fell on the ground at Jesus' feet and then, weeping, repeated Martha's complaint: "Lord, if you had been here, my brother would not have died." John notes how moved Jesus was by the tears of Mary and all the friends of the family who were present. Here we find the shortest verse in the Bible, only two words: "Jesus wept."

Finally Jesus approached the tomb, and here he ordered that the stone blocking its entrance be removed. Practical Martha warned him that there was bound to be an awful smell, but Jesus replied, "Did I not tell you that if you would believe you would see the glory of God?" At these words the stone was taken away. Jesus then lifted up his eyes and prayed for all to hear, "Father, I thank you that you have heard me. I know that you always hear me but I have said this on account of the people standing by that they might believe that you have sent me."

Finally, in a loud voice, he called into the tomb, "Lazarus, come out!" And he did, though wrapped from head to foot in strips of burial cloth. Jesus ordered the astonished witnesses, "Unbind him and let him go!"

John adds that not everyone who witnessed the miracle was pleased by it. Some went back to Jerusalem to report to the Pharisees, who in turn became more worried than ever about the danger Jesus posed and the possibility that he would unleash a chain of events that would result in the Romans destroying their country. Finally Caiaphas, the chief priest, declared, "It is better that one man die for the people so that the whole nation will not perish" (John 11:1–50).

The story of the raising of Lazarus, in which Christ's power over death itself was publicly displayed, was dear to the early Church. The earliest known versions of the icon, dating from the second century, are found repeatedly in the Roman Catacombs. The image is as simple as can be — Christ and Lazarus, face to face, the latter standing up in his winding sheet.

By the fourth century a more complex iconographic composition emerges that brings in much of the detail from John's Gospel. Mary (in red) and Martha are on the ground at the feet of Jesus while behind them a young man is removing the stone from the mouth of the tomb. The disciples of Jesus, Peter in the lead, stand behind the Lord. Witnesses stand near the tomb, gazing not at Lazarus but at him who can summon the dead back to life. Their covered hands are raised to their noses in expectation of the stench of death. Dominating the icon is Christ, a majestic figure, his right hand extended in a gesture of blessing toward Lazarus, seen rising from his coffin within a black cave. In the background we are given a glimpse of Jerusalem, where Jesus will suffer and rise from death. (*See color section.*)

Placing the two sisters in the center of the icon is a reminder that the Savior is moved by the tears of those who seek his help.

While there are many saints in the icon—Mary, Martha, and the Apostles — often there are halos around only two heads, Christ and Lazarus.

The two mountains in the background are associated with Mount Sinai and Mount Tabor, places where God was seen in glory. In Bethany too there was a revelation of God's glory, not in blinding light but in an action of which only God is capable.

"As a man you have wept over Lazarus," proclaims the Orthodox hymn of the feast, "and as God you have raised him."

Entry into Jerusalem

He who sits upon the throne of the cherubim, for our sake sits upon a donkey; and coming to his voluntary Passion, today he hears the children cry "Hosanna!"

— FROM AN ORTHODOX HYMN FOR PALM SUNDAY

Rulers of the ancient world would make their triumphal entrance into a city on a war horse. Jesus entered Jerusalem on a donkey. The meek creature, whose meek character is made more apparent in the icon by its lowered head, was perfect for a ruler without weapons, without armor, without an army. The Savior's manner of sitting astride the donkey also contrasts with an emperor riding his mount. It is not Caesar but the Prince of Peace entering into the Holy City. In this a prophecy of Zechariah is fulfilled: "Rejoice greatly, O daughter of Zion. Proclaim it aloud, O daughter of Jerusalem. Behold, your king is coming to you, triumphant and victorious, humble and riding on a donkey" (Zech. 9:9).

The icon is very simple — the Lord and his disciples to the left, the people welcoming him to the right, the wilderness behind the first group, the walled city behind the other, and a single tree between them.

The tree has a double meaning. By being pruned to provide branches for the crowd to wave at the Messiah, it suggests the "tree" outside the city walls to which the rejected Messiah will be nailed.

The joy of the city's welcome is suggested by the upraised palm branches the people carry, the children spreading garments (a sign of royal welcome) on the path, and the additional detail often found in the icon of several children cutting branches in the tree over Christ's head. In no other icon do children play so important a role.

The immediate cause of the crowd's welcome, the Evangelist John relates, was the miracle at Bethany, Jesus' raising of

Lazarus from the dead. Who but the long-awaited Messiah could call a corpse back to life? But we know from the same Gospel the state of dread the disciples were in as they approached Jerusalem. "Let us also go [to Jerusalem]," Thomas had said to the other disciples after failing to dissuade Jesus, "that we may die with him" (John 11:16).

The icon often draws attention to the fear and hesitancy of the Apostles by showing Christ directing his attention, not toward Jerusalem and those who await his entry with such excitement, but toward his disciples. We see them huddled together and notice that one of them — usually Peter — is in dialogue with the Lord, his hand extended as if making a final cautionary plea to his master.

Jesus' right hand is extended toward the city with a gesture of blessing while in his left a scroll represents his authority and also his awareness of what will happen — the crowd shouting, "Welcome to the son of David" will soon be the crowd screaming, "Crucify him."

Contemporary icon of the Holy Supper.

The Holy Supper

*"Take, eat, this is my body. Drink of it, all of you, for this is
my blood."*

— Matthew 26:26–28

Jesus promises those who follow him that they "will eat and
drink at my table in the kingdom" (John 12:30). In the eucharistic life of the Church, receiving Christ himself hidden in
bread and wine, we have already begun to do so.

In the background of the icon depicting the first eucharistic
meal, two buildings on either side are linked with a blood-red
cloth, a sign of the reconciliation of heaven with earth, God
with man, neighbor with neighbor.

In the foreground Christ presides, usually shown not at the
center but at the upper left of a circular table around which
the twelve are seated. It is the moment when Jesus has said,
"Truly, truly, I say to you, one of you will hand me over" (John
13:21).[51] We see Judas reaching into the bowl. (Another bowl
will appear later in the Passion narrative, but filled with water,
as Pilate, having condemned Jesus to death, washes his hands —
for no one wants to take upon himself the blame for murderous
actions.)

John, bowing toward the Lord, asks, "Lord, who is it?" Peter
is standing behind John saying, "Tell us who it is of whom he
speaks." Around a table, we find the Apostles in consternation,
as if echoing to each other the words of John and Peter.

We find heaven and hell in the same icon. Judas is physically
present at the holy table, in arm's reach of the Savior, but in
another sense he has made himself distant, for in his heart he
has abandoned Christ. He has become part of a conspiracy that
within hours will result in the arrest of Christ, his trial, torture,
and execution. So close and yet so far!

"Hell is not to love any more," wrote Bernanos. Despite all
we know about Judas, it isn't clear what led him to fall out of

love with Jesus, what fatal weakness Satan found in him, but a good guess is disappointment. Christ failed to measure up to Judas's expectations. Not only had he failed to overthrow the rulers and take their place, he had not even tried to do so. What had been the last straw for Judas was the anointing of Jesus with precious ointment by Lazarus's sister Mary in Bethany. Judas was scandalized that the money spent on the ointment hadn't been given to the poor. It may have seemed to him that Jesus wasn't living up to his own teaching. But Jesus sided with Mary. "Let her alone, let her keep it for the day of my burial. The poor you have always with you, but you do not always have me" (John 12:7-8). There are still those who share Judas's resentment of all extravagant acts of love and who are on guard against beauty.

Again and again we are reminded in the Gospel accounts that Jesus knew the hearts of those around him, knew their secrets and hidden intentions, but never on any occasion forced anyone's response. "Our God," Father Alexander Schmemann used to say, "is a God of freedom." We are free to love the Lord, as John does, or make ourselves the judge even of God himself, like Judas. We are free to choose heaven or hell.

Yet the Holy Supper icon is more about heaven than hell. The circular form of the table is the basic form of wholeness and suggests an infinity of spaciousness. There is a place at the table for anyone who wants to be there. We see too that heaven is not an abstraction in the future but is as real as a table, as real as bread and wine, and is open to us here and now in eucharistic life.

It is no wonder that, in the architecture of an Orthodox Church, the usual location for the icon of the Holy Supper is in the center of the iconostasis above the royal doors, directly in front of the altar. Under the icon the consecrated bread and wine is given to each communicant by name:

> The servant (handmaiden) of God, [*name*] receives the precious and holy Body and Blood of our Lord and God and Savior Jesus Christ, unto the remission of his (her) sins and unto life everlasting.

Crucifixion

Come, and let us sing the praises of him who was crucified for us. For Mary said, when she beheld him on the tree, "Though you must endure the cross, you are my son and my God."

— KONTAKION SUNG ON HOLY (OR GOOD) FRIDAY
DURING THE SERVICE OF THE TWELVE GOSPELS

All of us who are human beings are in the image of God. But to be in his likeness belongs only to those who by great love have attached their freedom to God.

— DIADOCHUS OF PHOTIKE

For those who see Jesus without the eyes of faith, his life was tragic. His first home was a cave. He spent part of his childhood as a refugee in Egypt. For several years he walked from place to place teaching a way of life that emphasized love of God and neighbor, but few became faithful followers. Finally he was executed for disturbing the religious establishment and the secular power. If this indeed were the entire story, the cross on which he died would represent nothing more than the ruthlessness of the state and the finality of death.

The first Christians would have been amazed that the cross would one day become a decorative object for sale in every jewelry store. For members of the early Church, living in a world in which the crucifixion of criminals and upstarts was a dreaded but not uncommon sight, the cross was an abrasive symbol, as chilling as the electric chair or hangman's rope is in ours. The shocking manner of Christ's death, Paul wrote, was "a stumbling block to Jews and foolishness to gentiles" (1 Cor. 1:23).

But it is "the holy and life-giving cross" that we see in the icon of the Crucifixion, the cross with which Christ defeated death and gave us the Resurrection.

When the Son of God became incarnate as Jesus, it was an act of divine *kenosis* —self-emptying love. Thus he hid his splendor. Even among the inner circle of those who accompanied him, only a few were permitted to see in him the glory of God. Absolute power was hidden in voluntary poverty. He was born in a shelter for animals, as an infant was pursued by soldiers seeking to kill him, as an adult had no home of his own, and only as a guest enjoyed the comforts of life. Entering Jerusalem for the last time, he stepped into the lion's jaws, knowing he would be arrested and aware of the violent death which would follow.

Western paintings since the Renaissance have put the emphasis on Christ's agony. The nails can hardly bear the weight of his bruised and blood-stained body. His mother and the other disciples at the foot of the cross are shown in a state of despair. Such paintings often include the two thieves crucified with Jesus as well as soldiers, scoffers, and passers-by, in whose faces we see a range of responses to Christ's suffering.

The Crucifixion icon, attending to the more hidden dimensions of the event and excluding all melodrama, stresses Christ's freedom and the gift he makes of himself. We see his non-resistance in his open hands and the lightness of his body on the cross. This is the heart of the icon. (The best known version of the Crucifixion icon in the Western Church is the one before which St. Francis of Assisi was praying when he heard Christ say to him, "Francis, rebuild my church." It comes from a more ancient model than the Russian icon reproduced here [*see color section*]. It was in the eleventh century that icons began to show Christ dead on the cross. In earlier icons his eyes were open.)

The anguish of those standing near the cross is understated. The icon includes only a few of those who were present. Christ's face is turned toward his mother, standing on the left. With Mary is one or several of the other women who followed Jesus. Mary is sometimes shown being supported by those around her. No less than the verbal accounts in the New Testament, the icon stresses the faithfulness of the women who joined Christ's community. Occasionally Mary's right hand is extended toward the Apostle John, on the right, as if to strengthen and reassure him in his struggle to endure his master's death.

The usual figure behind John is the centurion, included because he was moved to confess, "Truly this was the Son of God" (Matt. 27:54).

At the base of the cross is a small cave-like area containing a skull. Golgotha, the place of crucifixion outside Jerusalem's walls, means "the place of the skull." The tradition is that Adam was buried where Christ was later crucified. The theological meaning is that Christ is the new Adam who through his death on the tree of the cross has rescued us from the sin Adam and Eve committed under the tree of knowledge in Eden. The stone surrounding Adam's skull is split for, as the Gospel records, there was an earthquake at the moment Christ died.

The lower crosspiece to which Christ's feet were nailed (called a *suppedenium* by the Romans, it was a standard part of the cross) is sometimes angled so that one end is slightly higher. The raised side points toward the unseen good thief, who having confessed Christ, received the assurance that "today you will be with me in paradise" (Luke 23:43).

The icon has a Trinitarian structure. The three figures of Mary, Christ, and John give the icon a triangular inner composition reinforced by the arrangement of the rocks on which the cross is mounted and the peaked black space beneath. Bisecting the triangle is the vertical line of the cross, linking earth and heaven. The cross is revealed as the ladder to eternal life.

The icon shows Jerusalem's outer wall, not only because Christ was executed outside the city but as a reminder that those who follow Christ are exiles in this world. They can never be at home in the walled city of deceit, coercion and self-seeking. "For there is no lasting city for us in this life," wrote Paul (Heb. 13:11–14).

The upper part of Christ's body is placed above the wall, suggesting the cosmic significance of his death: "And when I am lifted up from the earth, I will draw everyone to myself" (John 12:32).

Like the Gospel authors, all the icons linked to Christ's suffering and death stress his love and freedom. He was not an unwitting victim but a free man.

If you trace the word "free" back to the ancient Indo-European language, the mother of modern Western languages, you arrive at the root word *"pri"* — "to love." The family of words of which "free" is a part includes "friend." In early English, "free" implied a relationship, meaning someone who was "dear to the chief" and who fought for his chief out of voluntary allegiance and love, not for money or out of fear. The free man was neither a conscript nor a mercenary. The free person is not our current Western image of the solitary cowboy on his horse in a desert "free" of all familial ties and responsibilities. To be free means that your ties are freely chosen because of your love for those people to whom you give allegiance. Genuine freedom implies sacrifice and submission.

In bearing the cross, we see Christ submitting to everything each of us fears and out of fear seeks to avoid: rejection, condemnation, humiliation, pain, failure, and death. He does so freely, with no motive but love for those with whom he has become one in the flesh. "Greater love has no man than to lay down his life for his friends" (John 15:13).

Resurrection

He descended into hell and on the third day he rose again.
— THE APOSTLES' CREED

Life fell asleep and hell shook with fear.
— A STIKHERON FOR HOLY SATURDAY

Enter then, all of you, into the Joy of our Lord. First and last, receive alike your reward. Rich and poor, dance together. You who have fasted and you who have not fasted, rejoice today. The table is fully laden: let all enjoy it. The calf is fatted: let none go away hungry. Let none lament his poverty; for the universal Kingdom is revealed. Let none bewail his transgressions; for the light of forgiveness has risen from the tomb. Let none fear death; for the death of the Savior has set us free.
— FROM THE PASCHAL SERMON OF ST. JOHN CHRYSOSTOM

"Christ is risen from the dead, trampling down death by death, and upon those in the tomb bestowing life." For forty days each year beginning with the midnight paschal service, Orthodox Christians sing this verse again and again until the words seem to drench us. No other proclamation better reveals the soul of Christian faith. It is the hymn of Pascha, and Pascha is the joy of all joys. The Church rejoices many times in the year — Annunciation, Christmas, Theophany, Ascension, Pentecost — but Pascha,[52] as the Orthodox call Easter, is *the* festival around which all the other feast days are gathered. Pascha is the most ancient of Christian festal events. From the beginning of the Church, the Resurrection was commemorated annually. All other seasons of remembrance were added later. Pascha is so much the center point of the church year that it isn't regarded simply as one of the twelve great feasts but rather "the eighth day of the week," the endless day that illumines the twelve, while every Sunday of the year is regarded as a "little Pascha," reflecting a fragment of the light shining from the empty tomb.

There are several paschal icons, each with its own emphasis, though none portrays the moment of Resurrection.

In one Christ is shown standing on a small cloud in front of the abandoned burial place while on either side are the sleeping soldiers, men whose closed eyes remind us of how blind we are most of our lives to God's presence.

Another icon portrays the first witnesses to Christ's Resurrection, the myrrh-bearing women who came to anoint the dead body of Christ but found an angel and the abandoned burial clothes. (*See color section.*) The tomb is placed in the background. "Why do you seek the living among the dead?" asks the angel (Luke 24:5). In a variation of the icon, Christ stands in the background, unnoticed except by Mary Magdalene. "The myrrh-bearing women anticipated the dawn and, like those who seek the day, they sought their Sun, who existed before the sun and who once submitted to the grave," an Orthodox hymn declares. "Then the radiant angel cried to them, 'Go and proclaim to the disciples that the Light has shone forth, awakening those who sleep in darkness, and turning tears into joy.' "[53]

The paschal icon most often painted by iconographers and most frequently found in Orthodox homes is the "Anastasis" — Christ's Descent into Hell. (*See color section.*) It is also the first paschal icon to be displayed in the center of the church each year, for it is venerated on Great and Holy Saturday.

The Apostles' Creed affirms that Christ "descended into hell" and this is what the icon shows us. Beneath his feet, falling into a pit of darkness, are the broken gates of hell, often shown as a cruciform platform upholding the Savior. "You have descended into the abyss of the earth, O Christ," the Church sings at Pascha, "and have broken down the eternal doors which imprison those who are bound, and like Jonah after three days in the whale, You have risen from the tomb."

The gates that seemed capable of imprisoning the dead throughout eternity are, through Christ's death on the cross, reduced to ruins. All others who have died have come to the land of death as captives, but Christ — in a golden robe and surrounded by a mandorla, a symbol of glory and radiant truth —

comes as conqueror and rescuer. (In some versions of the icon, there is a scroll in his left hand. When the inscription is shown, it reads, "The record of Adam is torn up, the power of darkness is shattered.") Beneath the gates of hell, only Satan and his servants are left in their kingdom of night and disconnection.

The principal figures to the left and right of Christ being raised from their tombs are the parents of the human race, Adam and Eve, while behind them are gathered kings, prophets and the righteous of Israel, among them David and Solomon, Moses, Daniel, Zechariah, and John the Baptist.

Chief among the dead who have been awaiting Christ are Adam and Eve, our mysterious original ancestors — so much like us! We live in a culture in which we're encouraged to find others to blame (and maybe sue) for our troubles — parents, teachers, neighbors, pastors, doctors, spouses, Hollywood, the mass media, big business, the government.... But self-justification by finger pointing is nothing new — Adam and Eve blamed the snake.

While not forgetting that there is truly much wrong with the structures we live in and thus much that we need to resist in this world, a very different way of looking at things is to focus, first of all, on our own failings. One of the tougher prayers in the Orthodox Church is the prayer we recite before receiving Communion. It begins, "I believe, O Lord, that you are truly the Christ, the Son of the living God, who came into the world to save sinners, of whom I am the first." Perhaps from a historian's point of view, I will not be listed among the all-time great sinners. But such a prayer helps me to stop making myself look relatively good by comparing myself to people who seem to be much worse, a nice method for finding myself not guilty by reason of comparative innocence.

If the failure of Adam and Eve in Paradise represents the primary catastrophe in human history from which all alienation, division, and cruelty have their source, surely this image of divine mercy toward them must be a source of consolation to everyone living in hope of God's mercy. "Delivered from her chains," comments an ancient paschal hymn, "Eve cries out in her joy" — and so may we.

It is only after his conquest of hell that Christ returns to his despairing disciples. "When He had freed those who were bound from the beginning of time," wrote the great defender of icons, St. John of Damascus, "Christ returned from among the dead, having opened for us the way of Resurrection."

The icon of Christ's Descent into Hell can be linked with an ongoing prayer not to live a fear-centered life. We live in what is often a terrifying world. Being fearful seems to be a reasonable state to be in — fear of violent crime, fear of job loss, fear of failure, fear of illness, fear for the well-being of people we love, fear of collapse of our pollution-burdened environment, fear of war, and finally fear of death. A great deal of what we see and hear seems to have no other function than to push us deeper into a state of dread. There were many elderly people who died in a heat wave in Chicago one summer simply because they didn't dare leave their apartments, for fear of muggers, in order to get to the air-conditioned shelters the city had provided. They died of fear.

We can easily get ourselves into a paralyzing state of fear that is truly hellish. The icon reminds us that Christ can enter not just some other hell but the hell we happen to be in, grab us by the hands, and lift us out of our tombs.

Ascension

When you had fulfilled for us your dispensation, and united the things on earth with the things of heaven, you, O Christ our God, ascended into glory, yet without being parted from those who love you, for you remain with them inseparably.

— FROM THE ORTHODOX KONTAKION
FOR THE FEAST OF THE ASCENSION

After a series of encounters with his disciples spread over forty days, the risen Savior was with them once again, this time at the top of the Mount of Olives, east of Jerusalem near the village of Bethany.

Even in their last face-to-face encounter with the Lord, the disciples' hopes still centered on restoration of the nation. He was asked, Luke records in the Acts of the Apostles, "Lord, will you at this time restore the kingdom of Israel?" (Acts 1:6). He responded not with the words they wanted to hear but with the promise that before long, with the descent of the Holy Spirit, they would finally understand that they were a part of something much vaster than their homeland. "You shall receive power when the Holy Spirit has come upon you, and you shall be my witnesses in Jerusalem and Judea and Samaria and to the ends of the earth."

Christ's Ascension is as mysterious an event as his Resurrection. Luke writes that as the disciples heard the promise of Pentecost,

> He was lifted up and a cloud took him out of their sight. And while they were gazing into heaven as he went, two men stood by them in white robes and said, "Men of Galilee, why do you stand looking into heaven? This Jesus, who was taken from you into heaven, will come in the same way as you saw him go into heaven" (Acts 1:10–11).

The Ascension icon has two tiers, heaven and earth. Usually the division is marked by a ridge of mountain peaks and olive trees, the branches of which are drawn upward by the Lord of Creation. (*See color section.*)

In the upper tier the glorified Christ, at the center of a mandorla of cosmic power, is lifted into heaven by the two angels of the Incarnation. He holds in his left hand the scroll of the Scriptures while his right is extended to bless those whom he has gathered. Here we see him ascending, but icons of the Last Judgment show him in the same way. In both cases we see him as being in eternity, presiding over history and judging it.

In the lower tier are the Apostles plus Mary. Her central role is made doubly apparent by her being placed in the middle and by highlighting her with the white robes of the two angels. In this arrangement we see her not only as the mother of the Savior but as the mother of the Church. She, who was God's bridge to the human race, is humanity's bridge to her son. In her we come closer to him. While the attention of the Apostles is divided, some watching the ascending Christ, others contemplating Mary, she is shown looking toward us. Her hands are sometimes shown being raised in prayer, at other times in the gesture linked with profession of faith. She alone among the disciples is calm, still, and silent.

Within the composition are two triangles, the base of each formed by the raised hands of the two angels. The peak of one is Christ's head, the peak of the other is between the feet of Mary. In this way the iconographer uses geometry to intensify the link between the principal figures.

The wide range of colors in the disciples' clothing suggests the universality of the Church, not the local institution the Apostles had expected, but a community whose members come from all nations. Some of the same colors are used for the robes of the two angels bearing Christ to heaven. The dominant colors of the icon as a whole are ivory and green, communicating a sense of peace and newness of life. This joyful icon seems to recite the words, "Behold, I make all things new" (Apoc. 21:5).

The angels said to the Apostles, "This Jesus, who was taken from you into heaven, will come in the same way as you saw him go into heaven." Rather than stare into the sky, his disciples are called to focus their attention on this world in order to prepare it for the Second Coming.

As the icon's composition reminds us, far from being abandoned, we have been provided with a community, the Church, the fountain of sacraments, in which those who follow Christ gather around the Mother of God, the first Christian.

The Descent of the Holy Spirit _____

When the Most High came down and confused the tongues, he divided the nations. But when he distributed tongues of fire, he called everyone to unity. Therefore with one accord we glorify the All-holy Spirit.

— Kontakion for Pentecost

The Holy Spirit provides all things: action, prophets well up like a spring; the Spirit installs priests; the Spirit makes theologians out of sinners; the Spirit gives being to the Church.

— A stikheron for Great Vespers

One of the surprising features of the New Testament is the candor of its portraits of the Apostles. Again and again we are shown their incomprehension, pettiness, ambition, and fear. While they were quick to recognize Jesus as the Messiah, the Messiah they eagerly awaited was a new King David. They saw Jesus as the man God had chosen to restore the unity and integrity of Israel and free it from foreign domination. What made the Galilean fisherman, Peter, chief of the Apostles (we often notice him in a primary position in icons[54]) was his realization that Jesus was not simply a great rabbi, leader, and prophet, but that he was God incarnate. "Who do you think I am?" Jesus asked. Peter responded, "You are the Christ, the Son of the Living God." But even Peter couldn't grasp the vastness of Christ's mission nor could he see anything but tragedy in Christ's death.

The only Apostle present at the Crucifixion was John; the rest had fled. Peter even denied he knew Jesus. The other disciples present at the foot of the cross were women, Christ's mother chief among them. Again, it was not the Apostles who went to the tomb to anoint Christ's body, but women — the Apostles were in hiding. The risen Jesus came to the Apostles, not the other way around. He met two other disciples (Luke and

The Savior of Zvenigorod, also known as Christ the Peacemaker
(by St. Andrei Rublev).

Christ Pantocrator.

The Annunciation.

The Transfiguration
(a contemporary icon by Protodeacon Paul Hommes).

The Raising of Lazarus.

The Crucifixion.

The Descent into Hell.

The Myrrh-bearing Women.

The Ascension.

The Holy Trinity
(by St. Andrei Rublev).

The Vladimir Mother of God.

Sts. Anne and Joachim
(a contemporary icon by Protodeacon Paul Hommes).

St. Sergius of Radonezh.

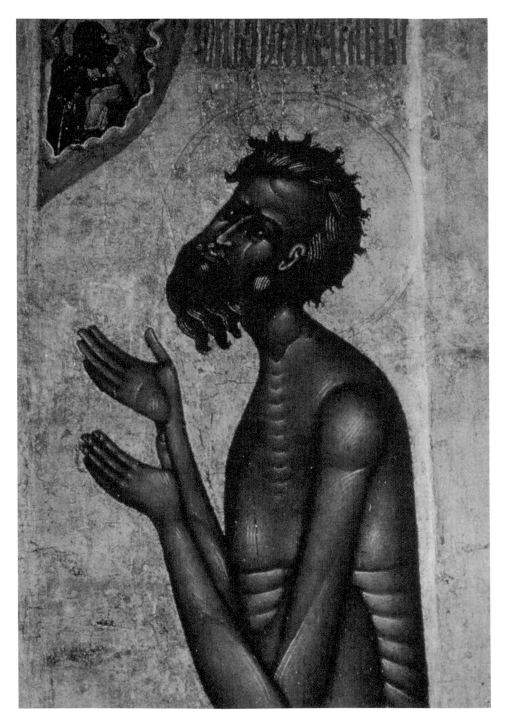

St. Basil the Blessed, Holy Fool of Christ.

Image of Christ "Made without Hands,"
also called The Holy Face.

A Russian iconostasis.

Cleopas, according to tradition) on the road out of Jerusalem and walked with them; they recognized the Lord only when he broke bread with them at the inn in Emmaus. Despite the witness of the others, despite the promises Jesus had made before his death, Thomas did not believe Christ had risen until he was able to touch the wounds in his body with his bare hands. Only then could Thomas make Peter's confession his own.

For forty days after the Resurrection there were encounters between Jesus and the Apostles, yet even then their perception of his purpose had enlarged only slightly. He reproached the Eleven, says Mark, "for their incredulity and obstinacy" (Mark 16:14).

Just before his Ascension, Jesus told the disciples that they would receive "power from the Holy Spirit" as a result of which they would become his witnesses "to the ends of the earth."

From the place of Christ's Ascension on the Mount of Olives, the band of followers walked back to Jerusalem to the upper room where they had been staying and began to pray continuously — the eleven Apostles, Mary the mother of Jesus, several other women, and several of Jesus' cousins. Occasionally they were joined by other followers of Jesus. It was in the upper room that the community elected Matthias to fill the place vacated by Judas, so that again there were twelve Apostles.

Their prayer continued for days. At last the event Jesus had promised occurred:

> Suddenly they heard what sounded like a powerful wind from heaven, the noise of which filled the entire house in which they were sitting, and something appeared to them which seemed like tongues of fire. These separated and came to rest on the heads of each of them. They were all filled with the Holy Spirit and began to speak foreign languages as the Spirit gave them the gift of speech. (Acts 2:1–4)

Immediately afterward Peter went out into the city to preach the Gospel and to announce the Resurrection of Jesus, speaking in such a way that everyone understood him despite many linguistic barriers — another work of the Holy Spirit. He spoke with such fearlessness that some witnesses thought he was drunk on "new wine." The event is celebrated as Pentecost, meaning the fiftieth day, on the seventh Sunday after the Resurrection. The icon of the Descent of the Holy Spirit summarizes the event with simplicity. The twelve sit on a semi-circular bench facing each other. The empty space at the top of the bench represents the unseen presence of the head of the Church, Christ, who promised he would remain with his followers "all days, until the end of the world." (In some versions of the icon, we find Mary sitting in this place, in her role as mother of the Church. When she is not included, it may be understood to imply that the fullness of the Holy Spirit, who descended into her with the Annunciation, was already hers.)

At the top of the icon is a partially revealed circle, a symbol of heaven, from which extend rays or flame shapes equal to the number of figures on the bench below. These represent the baptism of each person by the Holy Spirit. A longer ray, also representing the Holy Spirit, is sometimes shown emerging from the center of the sphere.

In no other icon do we see the Apostles in such a state of unity. The theme of the image is the unity which is impossible without the Holy Spirit. The Apostles are shown in inverse perspective; those who are farther away are slightly bigger than those in the foreground. Note that no figure is identical with any other. Through the variety of gestures and the range of colors, we are reminded that unity does not erase diversity.

The twelve are often shown in a non-historical way, with several of the Apostles who were actually in the upper room replaced by Paul and the Gospel authors Mark and Luke, for it was partly through them that the consequences of the Holy Spirit's descent at Pentecost reached "the ends of the earth." The evangelists and Paul are usually shown holding books. Others hold scrolls, a symbol of the Apostles' teaching office. When Paul is present, he sits on the top right, facing Peter. The place of Paul, Apostle to the Gentiles, is stressed because he saw more clearly than the others that no one is excluded from the Church. In response to Paul's missionary activities, Peter was given a dream in which he came to understand that "all things are clean" and that converts to Christ's way need not become Jews as well.

The icon makes no effort to suggest the sound of a roaring wind but rather the deep inner silence of the Apostles as they waited fulfillment of Christ's promise. Perhaps more than any other, this is an icon showing the condition of prayer — attentive waiting on the Lord.

The mysterious figure in the arched black space beneath the Apostles is Cosmos, symbol of all people in darkness awaiting illumination. He was made old by the sin of Adam and Eve. Though crowned with power and wealth, he is imprisoned in a cave of night awaiting conversion. In the white cloth in his hands he holds twelve identical scrolls, representing the light-giving teaching of the Apostles.

In some versions of the icon, in the place of Cosmos is the prophet Joel, whose foretelling of the future activity of the Holy Spirit was repeated by Peter when he preached his first sermon: "And it shall come to pass that I will pour out my Spirit on all flesh; your sons and your daughters shall prophesy, your old men shall dream dreams, and your young men shall see visions" (Joel 2:28; cf. Acts 2:14–41).

There is an Orthodox prayer associated with Pentecost, but recited and sung throughout the year, which is addressed to the Holy Spirit:

O Heavenly King, the Comforter, the Spirit of truth, everywhere present and filling all things, treasury of blessings and giver of life, come and dwell in us and cleanse us of every impurity and save our souls, O Holy One.

Holy Trinity

*God cannot be grasped by the mind. If God could be grasped,
God would not be God.*

— Evagrius of Pontus

*Let us love one another, so that with one mind we may confess
Father, Son, and Holy Spirit, the Trinity, one in essence and
undivided.*

— A prayer recited during the Orthodox Liturgy

The Holy Trinity icon expresses in silence aspects of the nature
of God beyond the reach of words. Every year on the feast of
Pentecost, it is placed in the center of the church, as this day
more than any other is linked to the revelation of the community of the Three within the One. Jesus' first followers, all Jews,
had known God the Father, creator of all things visible and invisible, from their childhood. In Jesus Christ the Savior, they
came to know God the Son. At Pentecost, they received the em-
powering gift of God the Holy Spirit, the Lord and giver of life,
intangible and yet present everywhere.

The icon refers to the story of Abraham and Sarah's hospitality to strangers by the oaks of Mamre near Hebron. Three
nameless visitors who appeared in front of their tent were
provided with food and drink, then they promised the aged
couple that barren Sarah would soon bear a son (Gen. 18).
Finally Abraham and Sarah understood their guests were angels. Throughout the biblical account the three acted in perfect
unity and spoke with one voice. In this the early Christian
community recognized a revelation of the Holy Trinity: three
Persons within the One God.

Earlier versions of the icon show Abraham and Sarah waiting on their guests. A later version painted by St. Andrei Rublev
(probably in 1425, five years before Rublev's death) drastically
simplified the image. Only the angels remain plus three objects

behind them: house, tree, and mountain. What had been a table with several dishes in earlier icons here becomes an altar with a chalice in the center. In stripping away narrative detail, Rublev shifted the icon's emphasis from a particular biblical event to a meditation on the dialogue of love within the Holy Trinity. (*See color section.*)

The icon was painted for the iconostasis of the principal church of the Holy Trinity Monastery north of Moscow. The monastery had been founded in the previous century by St. Sergius of Radonezh (1313–92), one of the towering figures in the history of the Russian Church. He left no books, but by word and example taught all who were drawn to his community in the forest that "contemplation of the Holy Trinity destroys all discord." The icon was intended to convey this teaching.

In the chronicles of the monastery it is remembered how on feast days, when St. Andrei and his assistant Daniel rested from their work, they would "sit in front of the divine and venerable icons and look at them without distraction.... They constantly elevated their thoughts to the immaterial and divine light."

The finished icon possessed an astonishing transparency, a serene, shimmering, heavenly beauty. It was quickly recognized as surpassing any previous icon on the same theme. In 1551, the Council of a Hundred Chapters cited it as a model, calling on iconographers "to paint from ancient models such as those made by the Greek iconographers and by Andrei Rublev."

"One can say without fear of contradiction," Paul Evdokimov has written, "that nowhere in the world is there anything like it from the point of view of theological synthesis, symbolic richness and artistic beauty."[55]

But the light of the icon slowly dimmed. As decades passed the smoke produced by thousands of candles blackened the image. Twice the image was repainted, but each time in darker colors and with the addition of new details. Finally the whole icon except the faces and hands was covered by a golden *oklad* —an embossed metallic sheet. What had once been visible in paint was rendered in cluttered relief.

It was only in 1904 that a restoration commission freed the icon from its *oklad* and began the slow and painstaking removal of the overpainting that masked Rublev's work. What their effort finally revealed has ever since amazed those who have been privileged to stand in front of the actual icon.[56] The uncovering of the Holy Trinity icon was a momentous event, doing much to inspire the return to classic iconography.

The miraculous grace of its colors and translucence defies even the most exacting efforts at reproduction.

The icon's principal colors were pure gold or hues of gold. Azure blue was used in the garments of the three figures with many touches in their robes of a wash of lapis lazuli. A thin line of vermillion was used for the hardly visible staff each figure holds. There is a small area of deep green in the tree and a wash of delicate mossy green in the figure to the right. The colors for the clothing of the central figure are the most substantial: deep red, dark blue, and a band of gold.

Apart from clothing, the three are identical. They are neither male nor female. The long bodies suggest a male form while the faces might be those of identical sisters. Each head is submissively inclined toward one of the others; none of the three assumes an imperial attitude. There is an atmosphere of love, freedom, timelessness, rest, and the most intimate communion. The sense of oneness is achieved primarily through the gentle, attentive engagement of the three with each other, the joining of eyes.

The structure of the icon contributes as well. Most important is the circle, symbol of perfection and eternity, created by the three figures; within the circle there is a sense of a slow counterclockwise movement. There is also a triangle, the peak of which is the head of the central figure.

Due to inverted perspective, there is no vanishing point. The three figures are not part of a disappearing plane but rather seem to move ever closer to the person before the icon, showing that God is here and everywhere.

Which angelic figure represents the Father, which the Son, which the Holy Spirit? There has been much debate on the question. When painted by Rublev, each figure was identified but the names were lost in the process of overpaintings and restoration. Some argue that the Son is represented by the figure in the center, but perhaps the best evidence is provided by a similar icon from the same period which belonged to

St. Stephen of Perm, a friend of St. Sergius and elder contemporary of Rublev. Here the angel on the left is identified as the Son, the angel in the center as the Father, the angel on the right as the Holy Spirit.

The three symbols at the top of the icon are each angled to mirror the angelic figures below them. At the center, above the Father, is a tree. What was the oak of Mamre becomes the Tree of Life planted by God in Paradise; beneath its branches Adam and Eve fell, but from it, according to tradition, the holy and life-giving cross was made. As a tree is linked with our downfall in the Garden of Eden, it is also linked with our salvation. Above the Son is a building without a door—the Church, open to all who seek sacramental life, in which we receive Christ in the Eucharist. Over the Holy Spirit there is a mountain—Mount Sinai, Mount Tabor, places where men have witnessed the glory of God.

Before the three figures is an altar on which stands a gold chalice containing, in miniature, a blood-red lamb's body symbolizing the sacrificial death of Christ, the Lamb of God. (Later in life, Abraham was to sacrifice a lamb in place of his son Isaac.) The Father's hand above the cup is extended in a gesture of blessing.

The image reminds us that, through the chalice, Christians are brought into communion with the Holy Trinity.

There is a sense of silent conversation among the three figures. The biblical text most often linked with their exchange comes from the Gospel of John: "God so loved the world that he gave his only begotten son, so that whoever believes in him should not perish but have everlasting life. For God sent his Son into the world, not to condemn the world, but that the world might be saved through him" (John 3:16–17).

If one were to search for a single word to describe the icon, it is the word "love." The Holy Trinity itself is a community of love so perfect that Father, Son, and Holy Spirit are one. All creation is a manifestation of God's love. The Incarnation of Christ is an act of love as is every word and action that follows, even if at times it is what Dostoevsky calls "a harsh and dreadful love." Christ's acceptance of condemnation and execution witnesses to the self-giving nature of love. His Resurrection is a sign of the power of love to defeat death. Christ invites each of us to participate in the love and mercy of God. "Love is the measure," said St. John of the Cross, "according to which we will be judged."

"Of all the philosophical proofs of the existence of God," wrote the priest and scientist Pavel Florensky, who died a martyr's death in the Stalin era, "that which carries the most conviction is not mentioned in any textbook. It may be summarized as follows: 'Rublev's Holy Trinity icon exists, therefore God exists.'"[57]

The Dormition of
the Mother of God

So intimately is the Mother of God bound up with the life of her son that, while she shared with him the experience of death and burial, soon afterward she was raised by him and brought to heaven to share in the divine glory. The icon joins the two separate but connected events, her death and resurrection. "Your grave and death," the Orthodox Church sings on the feast day, August 15, "could not keep the Mother of Life."

The image resembles the icon of Christ's Ascension. Here too Mary, mother of the Church, is in the lower center, no longer standing with upraised hands but lying in death, her eyes closed and hands crossed. Above her, within a mandorla representing heaven and wearing golden robes, Christ is holding his mother, wrapped in a burial sheet and represented as if she were a newborn child; roles reversed, she who once held the infant son in his swaddling cloth is now held by him. On either side of Mary's couch are the devoted Apostles plus several bishops — among them St. James, known as the brother of the Lord, the first bishop of Jerusalem, the city where the Church began.

In some versions of the icon an apocryphal scene is included in the foreground — Athonios, a non-believer, has dared to touch Mary's body, for which his hands are cut off by an angel. The detail is meant to suggest, comments Leonid Ouspensky, "that the end of life on earth of the Mother of God is an intimate mystery of the Church not to be exposed to profanation: inaccessible to the view of those without, the glory of the Dormition of Mary can be contemplated only in the inner light of tradition."[58]

Death is often spoken of in Orthodoxy as "falling asleep in the Lord." The word "dormition" means sleep. In the Roman Catholic Church the same event is called the Assumption.

This is a feast, comments Father Lev Gillet, "not only of Mary, but of all human nature, for in Mary, human nature reached its goal."[59]

Part IV

The Saints

Priest before an iconostasis in a Russian church.

Devotion to the Saints

Neither my wife nor I grew up in homes where icons had a place or where Mary was revered. In Nancy's case, growing up in a Dutch Reformed parish, Mary was hardly mentioned. To have a devotion to Mary was, by definition, something Catholic and therefore unthinkable. "One thing that was made very clear to us," Nancy recalls, "is that whatever we were, we weren't Catholics, still less Orthodox, which we hardly knew existed."

In Reformed thinking, you couldn't be a Protestant and have a devotion to any saint. The reasons behind this stance have much to do with commercial traffic in the relics of saints in the period that produced the Reformation. Many devout people in the age of Luther or Calvin saw that the Roman Catholic Church was giving more stress to saints than to Christ and the Bible. The abuses and distortions were real enough, but attempts to purify church life often resulted in overreaction. The baby was thrown out with the bath water.

Early in our marriage, Nancy asked if I could "explain" Mary to her. I burst out laughing. How could anyone possibly explain Mary? But I assured her that her question was a prayer and that Mary would answer it herself. And she has many times. For years Nancy has kept a small icon called "The Mother of God of the Sign" on her night table.

One of the aspects of Mary that Nancy admires is her freedom. She wasn't forced to bear Christ. The Archangel Gabriel appeared to her and asked if she were willing. "Be it done to me according to your word," she responded. No "yes" that was ever spoken had so much significance. Through Mary we have Christ. Through her flesh he took flesh. She gave birth to the Savior, nourished him, cared for him, raised him, and accompanied him as a disciple. She is linked with his first miracle, the transformation of water to wine at a wedding feast. She was at the foot of the cross when he was crucified. While dying, Christ called on the Apostle John to take care of her as if he were her son. Given her role in our salvation, is it surprising that the Orthodox Church speaks of her in the Liturgy as "more honorable than the cherubim and beyond compare more glorious than the seraphim"?

"The Church never separates Mother and Son, she who was incarnated by him who was incarnate" writes Father Sergius Bulgakov. "In adoring the humanity of Christ, we venerate his mother, from whom he received that humanity and who, in her person, represents the whole of humanity."[60]

From an early time Christians began to refer to her as the mother of the Church, finding in her a person who in every way provides a model of discipleship.

One of the earliest non-biblical texts about Mary, written about 90 C.E., is found in the Letters of St. Ignatius, bishop of Antioch: "And the virginity of Mary was hidden from the ruler of this world, as were her giving birth and likewise the death of the Lord —three secrets to be cried out aloud which were accompanied by the silence of God." Elsewhere he writes of the Lord being born "out of Mary and out of God."[61]

Late in the second century we find St. Irenaeus, the bishop of Lyon, describing Mary as the new Eve:

> Just as Eve, wife of Adam, yet still a virgin...became by her disobedience the cause of death for herself and the whole human race, so Mary, too, espoused yet a virgin, became by her obedience the cause of salvation for herself and the whole human race.... And so it was that the knot of Eve's disobedience was loosed by Mary's obedience.

For the fourth-century poet and hymn writer St. Ephraim the Syrian, Mary is "your mother, your sister, your spouse, your handmaiden."

Mary is found in many icons, most frequently simply holding Christ. Though the icons have numerous variations, always one hand gestures toward her son, the action that sums up her entire life to the present day. In some icons, his face is pressed against his mother's, an action of tender love and a reminder that his body was knit from her flesh. Mary is often depicted as the throne from which Christ reigns. Looking at the iconostasis, the screen of icons that marks the border between the main part of the church and the sanctuary, we find Mary in more than half the panels of the festal tier (the line of icons for the principal holy days). In the icon of Christ's Ascension, Mary stands in the very center of the community of believers, the Church.

The Church's attention to Mary was an integral part of its defense of the Incarnation. For the Gnostics, who sought redemption *from* the flesh, the flesh of Christ was a problem, for flesh in their view was synonymous with corruption and evil. For them Christ was not born of Mary but descended into Jesus, the son of Mary, at his baptism. Mary, therefore, was of no importance. Docetism, the most extreme form of the Gnostic heresy, denied that Christ had a truly human body; he simply appeared to have flesh.

For Orthodox Christianity, salvation was *of* the flesh, not from it, and icons served both as an affirmation of the Incarnation and of the significance of matter itself. "The title [of Mary as] Theotokos [God-bearer or Mother of God] contains the whole mystery of the Incarnation," wrote St. John of Damascus, the most articulate defender of icons.

Mary is the first and greatest of saints — "saint" meaning a person living in Christ for whom nothing takes priority over living out God's will. Such people are marked by love, courage, freedom, and obedience. They are whole, and for this reason we call them holy. The family of words to which holy belongs includes "whole," "wholesome," "healthy," and the Old English word for Savior, *Hælend*.[62] The halos placed around the heads of saints in icons suggest the light of Christ that shines through them. Each saint in a unique way reveals something about who Christ is. In some way each saint draws us closer to Christ.

Most of the saints of the early Church were martyrs, so named from the Greek word for witness; they gave witness by shedding their blood, not that they sought death but that they would rather die than deny or compromise their faith in Christ. The places they were buried quickly became places where the local church celebrated the Liturgy of the Eucharist. Reverent care for the bodies of those who died for the faith was a hallmark of the Church from its first days. "The blood of the martyrs is the seed of the Church," wrote Tertullian early in the third century.

"Since we are surrounded by so great a cloud of witnesses," wrote St. Paul, "let us also lay aside every weight and sin which clings so closely, and let us run with perseverance the race that is set before us" (Heb. 12:1).

The cloud of witnesses is the communion of saints: all those who have given an example of heroic perseverance in the race toward the Kingdom of God. People without faith regard the saints as dead and gone, but the Church declares that we find in Christ all those whose life was Christ. The saints are not simply remembered as having once set a good example but they become our companions in day-to-day life. One of the earliest definitions of the Church was the Communion of Saints. They are near to us, nearer than we imagine.

I think of a surprising letter I received in 1994 from my Lutheran friend Bobbie Stewart, whose church tends to regard devotion to Mary or any other saint with alarm. She had gone to Mexico to take part in a theological seminar, but the great event of her visit occurred at the basilica commemorating the appearance of Our Lady of Guadalupe to an Aztec Indian in 1531.

"Once inside the church," she wrote, "I said a prayer to Our Lady. And sitting there, I felt I was surrounded and then infused with this incredible love. I knew that Mary held me in her heart — and I knew that she held all of us in her heart. And for the first time I understood — beyond words — how God could care for each of us. I always believed God loves us all, but there are so many of us that I never figured God could really notice or attend to each of us as individuals. But having experienced how Our Lady does it, I could begin to understand that God can. Bringing this experience back from Mexico has made me feel a consciousness that each person I meet, and everyone I see on the street, is held in Mary's heart, so I try to look at them that way. I don't always succeed, but I keep working at it."

I recall another experience involving a Protestant friend, Hannes de Graaf, who taught for many years at the University of Utrecht. As a young man his interest in the novels of Dostoevsky led him to learn Russian, a language which he put to good use later in life, during the Cold War, when he would occasionally travel to Russia on behalf of the International Fellowship of Reconciliation.

One day he was in an Orthodox Church in Moscow standing in front of an icon of Mary and Christ when an old Russian woman approached him. She could see at a glance that Hannes was a foreigner. Few Russians could afford such clothing. And she could see he wasn't Orthodox — he hadn't crossed himself, he hadn't kissed the icon. He was looking at it as one might look at a painting in a museum. "Where do you come from?" she asked. "Holland," Hannes replied. "Oh, yes, Holland. And are there believers [as Russians refer to Christians] in Holland?" "Yes, most people in Holland belong to a church." He could see the doubt in her face.

She began to cross-examine him. "And you also are a believer?" "Yes, in fact I teach theology at the university." "And people in Holland, they go to church on Sunday?" "Yes, most people go to church. We have churches in every town and village." "And they believe in the Father, Son, and Holy Spirit?" She crossed herself as she said the words. "Oh, yes," Hannes assured her, but the doubt in her face increased — why had he not crossed himself? Then she looked at the icon and asked, "And do you love the Mother of God?" Now Hannes was at a loss and stood for a moment in silence. Good Calvinist that he was, he could hardly say yes. Then he said, "I have great respect for her." "Such a pity," she replied in a pained voice, "but I will pray for you." Immediately she crossed herself, kissed the icon, and stood before it in prayer.

"Do you know," Hannes told me, "from that day I have loved the Mother of God."

A large book could be devoted simply to icons of the saints — they number in the thousands. In this small volume there is room only for a sampling: two of the many icons of Mary plus several of other saints whose images are to be found in churches and homes.

The Mother of God of Tenderness.

The Mother of God of Tenderness ____

Mary's was a sublime beauty, making both worlds beautiful.[63]
— St. Gregory Palamas

One of the most frequently painted of all icons reminds us of the love that binds Mary and Jesus to each other, and also of the connection between Mary and ourselves, for we too are her children. There are numerous variations, but all of them show Christ in his mother's arms with their faces pressed together. One of her hands holds him, the other draws our attention to him, a motion reinforced by the gentle tilt of her head. There is often a subdued sense of apprehension in Mary's face, as if she can already see her son bearing the cross, while Christ seems to be silently reassuring his mother of the Resurrection.

This is one of the icons attributed to the Gospel author Luke. While we know with certainty of no surviving icon painted by his hand, according to tradition the original of this icon was his.

The most famous version of the icon, the Vladimir Mother of God, was given by the Church in Constantinople to the Russian Church in about 1131. (*See color section.*) Every movement and use of the Vladimir icon has been chronicled ever since. It was in Kiev until that city was destroyed by the Golden Horde. From there, in 1155, it went to the city of Vladimir in the north. In 1395 the icon moved once again, this time to Moscow, a river town that had grown into the chief city of Russia.

At present the icon is behind a screen of thick glass in Moscow's Tretyakov Gallery, though on one occasion, in a moment of national crisis in 1993, it was taken out of the museum by the head of the Russian Orthodox Church, Patriarch Alexei, and used to bless the city — the kind of action long associated with this icon. Even in the museum, it is not unusual to see people in fervent prayer as they stand before this battered image. (There are many good printed reproductions of the Vladimir icon but nothing I have seen does justice to the original. Partly this is because the surface of the icon, having suffered much damage, reveals level upon level of the overpainting of those who restored the icon over the centuries. We see portions of earlier painting in one area, later retouching in others. The rough terrain of the icon's surface is lost in prints.)

In some versions of the icon — the Vladimir prototype is one — Mary appears to be looking toward the person praying before the icon; in others her gaze is slightly off to the side, but in either case her eyes have an inward, contemplative quality. "The Virgin's eyes," Henri Nouwen comments, "are not curious, investigating or even understanding, but eyes which reveal to us our true selves."[64]

Invariably Christ's attention is directed to his mother. Always there is the detail of Christ's bare feet, a vivid symbol of his physical reality: he walked among us, leaving his footprints on the earth.

In some versions of the icon there is an additional detail of love, the arm of Christ around his mother's neck. This too is in the Vladimir prototype.

In contrast to Renaissance religious paintings with a similar subject, we notice in the icon that while Christ is an infant in size, his body's proportions are those of a man; a baby's head would be much larger. This is intentional. The noble face we see pressed against Mary's cheek is the Lord of Creation and the Glory of God. He wears adult clothing, a tunic and coat woven from gold, the color iconography uses for the imperishable and all that is associated with the Kingdom of God. In these details the icon reveals the real identity of the son of Mary.

Over her dress, Mary wears a dark shawl which circles her head, has a golden border, and is ornamented with three stars (one is hidden by Christ's body) symbolizing her virginity before and after her son's birth. At the same time they suggest that heaven has found a place in her.

The icon's triangular composition not only emphasizes the stillness of the two figures and gives the icon an immovable solidity but is a reminder of the presence of the Holy Trinity in all things.

The center of the composition is at the level of Mary's heart. A much-used Orthodox prayer declares, "Beneath your tenderness of heart do we take refuge, O Mother of God." As anyone discovers in coming to know the Mother of God, her heart is as spacious as heaven.

In any version of the icon of the Mother of God of Tenderness, the Vladimir icon being only the most famous example, we see Mary's perfect devotion, a devotion so absolute that God finds in her the person who can both give birth to himself and who will ever after serve as the primary model of Christ-centered wholeness — the woman whom all generations will regard as blessed. In her assent to the angelic invitation, Mary said not only on behalf of herself and all her righteous ancestors but for all generations, "Yes, Lord, come!" Through her all humanity gives birth to Jesus Christ, and through Christ she becomes our mother.

Because the icon portrays the profound oneness uniting Mary and Jesus, it is a eucharistic icon: in receiving the Body of Christ, we too hold Christ, and are held by Christ.

In the Gospel, we hear Mary praised for having given birth to Jesus and having nursed him. Christ responds by remarking on what is still more important about his mother and all who follow him wholeheartedly: "Rather blessed are they who hear the word of God and keep it" (Luke 11:28). She who gave birth to the Word of God also keeps it eternally.

It was at Mary's appeal that Christ performed his first miracle, changing water into wine at the marriage feast at Cana, and at Cana that we hear her simple appeal to each person who would follow her son: "Do whatever he tells you" (John 2:5). These few words would serve well as another name for this icon.

Icon of the Mother of God of the Sign.

The Mother of God of the Sign _____

*Therefore the Lord himself will give you a sign. A virgin will
conceive and bear a son and shall call him Immanuel.*

— Isaiah 7:14

*And far beneath the movement of this silent cataclysm Mary
slept in the infinite tranquility of God, and God was a child
curled up who slept in her and her veins were flooded with
His wisdom which is night, which is starlight, which is silence. And her whole being was embraced in Him whom she
embraced and they became tremendous silence.*[65]

— Thomas Merton

One of the most ancient icons is the Mother of God of the Sign,
the earliest known example of which is found in the Roman
Catacombs. Mary is in the classical posture of prayer, standing with upraised hands, facing the person praying before the
icon. Within her, often contained in a heaven-like circle, we see
Christ revealed, shown not as an unborn child curled up in his
mother's womb, but as Christ Immanuel, "God with Us," vested
in golden robes and looking outward while his right hand offers
a blessing.

When placed in an iconostasis that includes a tier of icons
of the prophets, this icon is placed in the center, for through
Mary the prophecies of redemption were at last realized. Mary,
the daughter of Israel, is the virgin Isaiah saw in the distance
of time.

It is an icon of circles, symbols of wholeness and perfection.
Mary's torso has a circular quality, as do the heads of both
figures. There is the circle around Christ. The two halos are
circular. Mary's hands are arched as if holding up a still larger
circle.

In a society in which abortion has been widely accepted, the
icon acquires a prophetic significance. The unborn Christ, al-

though his presence was unknown to anyone but his mother, was nonetheless incarnate and physically present in the world from the moment of his conception. No wonder one of the earliest prohibitions made by the Church was directed at abortion. The icon invites us to a deeper reverence for life.

The icon reminds us of the words of St. Paul, "It is no longer I who live but Christ who lives in me" (Gal. 2:20). While Mary is uniquely the Savior's mother, it is as his faithful disciple that she serves as the primary model of a Christ-centered life. More than that, like Mary, we uncover the secret of who we are in discovering Christ at the center of our lives.

Sts. Anne and Joachim

The mother of the Messiah was the only child of Joachim and Anne, who met and married in Jerusalem. Like Abraham and Sarah, they had to wait for decades for a child until Anne was past her child-bearing years. Still they prayed, vowing that if they were blessed with either son or daughter, they would offer their offspring as a gift to the Lord. After the promise was made, an angel appeared to Anne, announcing she would bear a daughter "whose name would be proclaimed throughout the world and through whom all nations would be blessed." Soon after Mary's birth, Joachim and Anne brought her to the Temple in Jerusalem to offer her to God. According to tradition, the couple lived long lives, Joachim until he was eighty, Anne until she was seventy-nine.[66]

"God is love," St. John the Evangelist declares. We see in the gentle embrace portrayed in the icon not only the love that joins Joachim and Anne in marriage but we glimpse the deliverance of the world in the love which unites the grandparents of the Savior. So much depended on their devotion to each other and to God.

In modern writing about the nativity of Christ, some authors reject the Gospel account of his virgin birth not only because they object to miracles in general but because they see a pregnancy occurring through the Holy Spirit's intervention as diminishing procreation within marriage. The problem is made more complex because in the history of Christianity, especially in the West, celibacy has often been presented as a higher vocation, with marriage and sexual life between husband and wife as something only to be grudgingly tolerated.

This icon reveals a very different attitude. We see in it a celebration not only of the sanctity of the parents of Mary but a ringing affirmation of the vocation of marriage. Here Joachim is the ideal husband and Anne the perfect wife. The meek submission of each to the other in love is suggested in the slight bending not only of Anne toward Joachim but of Joachim toward Anne. Their faces touch while the two arms visible in the image make a crossing gesture similar to the gesture associated, in Orthodox practice, with receiving communion. There is another remarkable detail: Anne's outer garment seems blown open not by a strong wind but by the inner opening of Anne to her beloved. Though husband and wife are clothed in the most modest way one can imagine, the icon communicates a climate of the deepest intimacy. (*See color section.*)

In some versions of the icon we find a single building behind the two, suggesting the miraculous unity that can occur within marriage. In other versions, there are two houses, one behind Joachim, the other behind Anne, both with open doors, with the two connected by a red banner draped between the roofs: another symbol of separation overcome — between man and woman, but also between humanity and the Creator.

Archangels

Bless the Lord, O you his angels, you mighty ones who do his word, hearkening to the voice of his word!

— PSALM 103:20

For the Son of Man is to come with his angels in the glory of the Father....

— MATTHEW 16:21

According to tradition, on the first day of creation, the day of light, God made the nine orders of bodiless creatures. They were in three ranks: first Cherubim, Seraphim, and Thrones; then Dominions, Virtues, and Powers; and finally Principalities, Archangels, and Angels. We find frequent mention of them in the Bible, from the Book of Genesis to the Apocalypse.

Their role in human history is central. The creation of Adam and Eve caused division among the angelic host, some of whom — Lucifer chief among them — were unwilling to pay homage to beings they considered beneath themselves. From that moment, the angelic powers that joined Lucifer, allying themselves against God and the human race, have been the hidden actors in every evil deed, from deceit to genocide. "We struggle," wrote St. Paul, "not against flesh and blood but against Powers and Principalities."

Those angelic beings who remained faithful have, in their endless worship of God, ever since been bound up with safeguarding creation and seeking the salvation of each human being, because we are icons created in the image and likeness of God.

Seven of the Archangels loyal to God are known to us by name: Michael, the archangel of struggle against evil; Gabriel, the archangel of truth; Raphael, the archangel of healing; Uriel, the archangel of conversion; Selephiel, the archangel of wisdom; Varachiel, the archangel of courage in the face of

119

An angel.

persecution; and Yegovdiel, the archangel of unity. Through encounters with angels, we apprehend aspects of God.[67]

The archangels we see most often in icons are Michael and Gabriel, messengers (in Greek, *angelos*) appearing at pivotal events having to do with the salvation of the world.

In connection with the birth of John, Gabriel appeared to Zechariah, and six months later to Mary, in both cases announcing events that could be realized only through the free response of those to whom God's will was revealed.

In the Apocalypse we find Michael leading the angelic host in the celestial battle against the "dragon" (Lucifer, or Satan) and those loyal to him, a war we experience daily in this world though we can only see its consequences, not its actors. "The demons," the poet and translator Richard Pevear comments, "are visible only in distortions of the human image, the human countenance, and their force is measurable only by the degree of this distortion."[68]

As insubstantial beings, angels can be portrayed only in a symbolic way. Their qualities are represented with material forms. We see them as beautiful beings because, in their love of God, they reflect the beauty of God. Though more ancient than the stars, we see them as young because God "makes all things new" (Apoc. 21:5). They are given long, eagle-like wings to show that instantly they will go wherever they are needed by God. Their intelligence and absolute attention are reflected in the facial expressions assigned to them. The decorative ribbons in their hair, the ends of which flow from either side of their heads, symbolize obedient listening to God's voice. Their feet hardly touch the ground, reminding us they are not material beings. Occasionally an archangel is given one or more objects that symbolize its special function. Thus Michael is often shown wearing armor and carrying a sword.

In biblical accounts of human encounters with these magnificent beings, it is striking how often we hear the words, "Be not afraid." No doubt it is terrifying to see an angel. Reassurance must be needed; but beyond that, angels are associated with our overcoming all those paralyzing fears which prevent each of us from living a God-centered life.

St. John the Forerunner _____

Described by Christ as "more than a prophet," St. John the Forerunner (or the Baptist) has been regarded by the Church as second only to Mary in the community of saints. Though John was the natural child of Elizabeth and Zechariah, his birth had a miraculous dimension as his mother was above child-bearing age and had been barren. "Many will rejoice in his birth," Zechariah was told by the Archangel Gabriel, "and he shall be great before the Lord." Even before his birth, John had leapt in his mother's womb when Mary, bearing Jesus, came to visit her cousin, Elizabeth. It was John who prepared Israel for the Messiah by baptizing them in the Jordan,[69] and it was John who first recognized Jesus as the Messiah, confessing that he "was not worthy to untie his sandal." He died a martyr's death for condemning Herod's immorality. The celebration of the anniversary of his death, commemorated on June 24, is one of the most ancient fixed dates on the church calendar.

Apart from the festal icon of the Theophany or Baptism of Christ, there are two icons of St. John common to Orthodox churches.

One is intended to be part of a group of three, with the Mother of God on the left, Christ in the center, and John on the right. John's head, like Mary's, is tilted meekly toward the Savior, while one or both hands are extended in a gesture of prayer or petition. In some versions of the icon, John's right hand holds a scroll with the text, "Repent, for the Kingdom of Heaven is at hand." The three icons are placed at the center of the Deisis (or intercession) tier when it is included in an iconostasis.

In another icon type, we see John with wings, the angelic symbol meaning that John was a messenger (*angelos*) of God. The reference is to the words of Jesus, "This is he of whom it is written, Behold, I send my messenger before your face, who shall prepare your ways before him" (Matt. 11:10). The wilderness that was John's home is sometimes seen in the background. In one of his hands, or in the foreground of the icon, is a plate with John's head, the price he paid for speaking the truth fearlessly before the rulers.

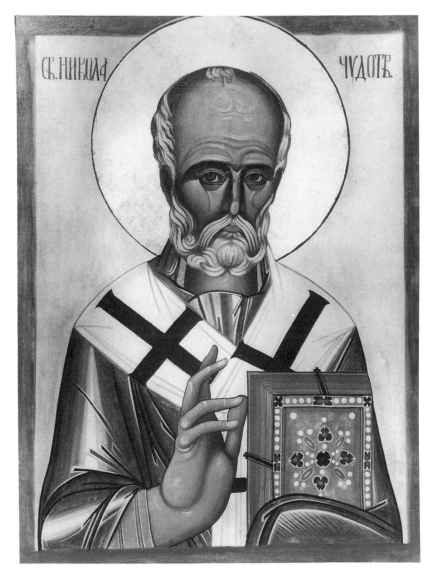

St. Nicholas.

St. Nicholas the Wonderworker _____

An astonishing number of churches are named in honor of St. Nicholas, a fourth-century bishop of Myra, a city now in ruins in Asia Minor (modern Turkey). He wrote no books nor have any of his sermons or letters survived, but few saints have been the object of such universal affection. He is seen as a brave defender of Orthodoxy, a model pastor, a protector of the poor and defenseless, a guardian of children. He is the patron of seafarers, prisoners, and orphans. No other saint has been so often represented in icons except the Mother of God. "Having fulfilled the Gospel of Christ...you have appeared in truth as a most holy shepherd to the world," the Orthodox Church sings on his feast day, December 6.

Born about 280, Nicholas was the only child of wealthy parents, citizens of Patara in Lycea, who arranged for their son to receive a Christian education from his uncle, the bishop of Patara. Taking literally the words of the Gospel, when his parents died, Nicholas distributed their property to the poor, keeping nothing for himself. Though drawn to a solitary monastic life, he felt led by God's will to service as a priest in the world. Soon after his ordination, he was chosen as archbishop of Myra. Shortly before his election, Nicholas is said to have had a vision of Christ handing him the Gospel book and the Mother of God placing on his shoulders the bishop's *omophorion.*[70]

During the persecutions of Diocletian and Maximian at the end of the third century, he was among the many thousands imprisoned and tortured, but even in chains carried on his pastoral and teaching work.

Following Emperor Constantine's Edict of Tolerance in 313, Nicholas was among the bishops participating in the First Ecumenical Council at Nicea in 325, where, according to legend, he was so angered by the heretic Arius, who denied that Jesus was the Son of God, that he struck him on the face. For his emotional act, he was removed from the Council and for a short time was barred from episcopal service.

Restored to his office as archbishop of Myra, on one occasion he saved three men from execution, physically restraining the astonished executioner. Stories link him with the release of other men unjustly imprisoned. Tireless in his care of people in trouble or need, he was regarded as a saint even during his lifetime. At times, it is said, his face shone like the sun.

He died on December 6, 343, and was buried in Myra's cathedral. In the eleventh century, his relics were brought to Bari, Italy, where they remain.

The icons of St. Nicholas are usually full-face views in which we glimpse his kindness, his attentiveness, and his strength of faith — qualities of the ideal pastor.

St. George
the Dragon Slayer _____

According to legend, a dragon lived in a lake in the region of Cappadocia in Asia Minor and was worshiped by the terrified local people, who fed him their children to subdue the dragon's rage. When it was the turn of Elizabeth, the king's daughter, to be sacrificed and she was going toward the lake to meet her doom, St. George appeared riding a white horse. He prayed to the Father, Son, and Holy Spirit, then transfixed the dragon with his lance, and afterward led the vanquished creature into the city. The wounded monster followed Elizabeth, says the *Legenda Aurea* of Blessed James de Voragine, "as if it had been a meek beast." Afterward George called on the local people to be baptized.

Such wonderful tales came centuries after George had died a martyr's death. The real dragon George fought against was panic. Living in the time of the persecutions of Diocletian and Maximian, when many Christians were being arrested and taken away to torturers and executioners, he had the courage to walk into a public square and shout, "All the gentile gods are devils. My God made the heavens and is the true God." For this he was arrested and put to death. His witness is said to have led to the conversion of many and given courage to others who were already baptized.

Like Nicholas of Myra, St. George is a deliverer of prisoners and protector of the poor. Perhaps because his name means "husbandman," he is also the patron of agriculture, herds, flocks, and shepherds.

The icons of St. George slaying the dragon are simple but powerful images of the struggle against evil and fear, represented by the dragon. The white horse St. George rides is a graceful creature as light as air and as fearless as his rider. The thin cross-topped lance the saint holds is not tightly grasped but rests lightly in his hand — meaning that it is the power of God, not the power of man, that overcomes evil. George's face shows not a trace of anger, hatred, or anxiety. Often the hand of the Savior is extended from heaven in a sign of blessing.

St. Sergius of Radonezh _____

An hour's drive north of Moscow is the Holy Trinity–St. Sergius Lavra, a monastic enclave which has long been one of the great centers of the Russian Orthodox Church. In 1334, when the region was heavily forested, St. Sergius of Radonezh and his brother Stephen erected a small wooden church here, dedicating it to the Holy Trinity, and built two log cabins nearby.[71] The solitude, austerity, and hunger proved too much for Stephen, who rejoined an urban monastic community, but his younger brother remained alone in what he regarded as the "desert."

As the years passed, a few others were attracted to the poor way of life Sergius was following. Gradually a large community came into being. None of the growth was planned or desired by Sergius. He accepted everything as God's will, even his own election as abbot and ordination as a priest, though to the end of his life, by which time the community was receiving many gifts, he wore a vestment of rags — a disappointing spectacle to some of those who came to meet him. Within the monastic community, he preferred the lowliest tasks.

From his early years of solitude in the forest, Sergius formed a long-lasting association with a bear who visited him daily, always receiving a portion of bread. Sometimes, when there wasn't enough bread for the two of them, Sergius gave all his bread to the bear, explaining to the younger monks, "I understand fasting, but the bear does not."

In 1422, twenty-four years after his death, a cathedral church of stone replaced the wooden structure, and St. Andrei Rublev's icon of the Holy Trinity was painted for the iconostasis.

For more than six hundred years, the church has been a place of pilgrimage. Every morning, several monks begin a service of prayer there, but pilgrims soon start to arrive and before long they take over the service, which continues without interruption until nightfall. It is a dark church, the only light coming from candles clustered near several icons and especially near the tomb of the saint whose relics are venerated by all who are drawn to the Lavra.

There is a chapel-like structure near the cathedral built over a well. Here water began to flow miraculously during the lifetime of St. Sergius and has ever since been associated with healing. The water tastes like fresh melted snow.

"This Lavra is the center of the Russian Orthodox Church, and St. Sergius is the heart of the Lavra," Father Alexei, a young monk, told my wife and me when we came as pilgrims in 1987. "His heart encompasses the whole world."

We were shown several objects linked with St. Sergius — two chalices made of wood, several small icons, one of his sandals, and a tool he used in making wooden toys.

There are still experiences at the Lavra of people encountering St. Sergius, said Father Alexei. "In one case a pilgrim came from a remote part of the country and had made no arrangements to stay anywhere for the night. It began to rain. An old man in rags came up to him and asked, 'Why are you standing in the rain? Please join me.' They walked for fifteen minutes to a small log cabin where the old man gave his guest bread and water and a bench to sleep on. When the man woke in the morning, the pilgrim discovered he was under a fir tree. He told the monks what had happened. They knew that St. Sergius himself had once again cared for another pilgrim."

St. Sergius wrote no books. None of his talks were written down. If he sent any letters, none survives. What we know of his teaching comes chiefly from what a biographer in the next generation wrote, "St. Sergius built the Church of the Holy Trinity as a mirror for his community, that through gazing at the Unity, they might overcome the hateful divisions of this world."

The icon of Sergius, found in every Russian church, is as quiet and modest as the saint himself, revealing his purity of heart and complete devotion to God. (*See color section.*)

St. Seraphim of Sarov _____

To the degree that love for the Lord warms the human heart, one finds in the Name of Jesus a sweetness that is the source of abiding peace.

— St. Seraphim of Sarov

It was Father Ghermann, a monk I met in the Russian city of Vladimir, who first told me about St. Seraphim of Sarov. He was showing me the local cathedral, still a museum in those days of Soviet rule. The tourists in the church were startled to see a living monk complete with long hair, full black beard, and black monk's cap — they couldn't stop staring. It wasn't only his appearance that attracted attention. He possessed a contagious joy and freedom. I mentioned to him that this church must have wonderful acoustics. Immediately he sang an unrestrained, banner-like, "Amen." The church reverberated in an astonishing way.

I had traveled enough in Russia to be vaguely aware of St. Seraphim, the icon of whose compassionate face graced the walls of every parish church, but Father Ghermann was the first to tell me the saint's life story.

"St. Seraphim helped me to become a believer," he said. He showed me a fragment of a large rock on which St. Seraphim prayed for a thousand days. It was a gift from an old nun who knew a nun who knew a nun who had been in the Diveyevo convent near Sarov, a community closely linked with St. Seraphim. The saint's few possessions, among them the heavy cross he wore, were kept in the custody of the sisters at Diveyevo.

Father Ghermann explained that Seraphim was born in 1759, the son of a builder. He was still a baby when his father died. His mother took over the business while raising her children. Still a boy, he had what should have been a fatal fall from scaffolding, which left him unharmed, an event which prompted a local "holy fool" to say the boy must surely be "one of God's elect."

131

St. Seraphim (a contemporary icon by Philip Zimmerman).

When he was ten, he had his first vision of the Mother of God. Nine years later he entered monastic life, where he began his practice of the Jesus Prayer: "Lord Jesus Christ, Son of God, have mercy on me, a sinner." Later, following his ordination as priest in 1793, he was led to seek a hermit's vocation in the forest, or, as he regarded it, his "Holy Land." Here he lived alone, devoting himself to prayer, study, and tending his small garden, with few aware he was alive apart from the wild animals he befriended with gifts of food, among them a bear who sometimes lay at his feet, a scene portrayed in some of the icons of St. Seraphim. During this period of social withdrawal, he was nearly beaten to death by robbers who had heard there was a treasure hidden in his cabin; the injuries he suffered made him walk with a bent back for the rest of his life, a stance occasionally shown in icons. After recovering from his injuries, he spent a thousand days and nights in prayer on a large rock in the forest, sometimes standing, other times kneeling, leaving the rock only for brief periods.

After his long apprenticeship in solitude, people began coming to *Staretz*[72] Seraphim for confession and advice, a few at first, but finally they came in floods. One of the first pilgrims was a rich man, gravely ill, who was healed by Seraphim, so healed that he gave up all his wealth and embraced holy poverty. During the last eight years of his life, St. Seraphim spent many hours each day talking with those in need, some of whom had walked for weeks to reach him. Others came by carriage, among them Tsar Alexander I, who later gave up the throne and lived a pious life in Siberia — some say under the influence of St. Seraphim.

Among many remarkable stories left to us about Seraphim's life, one of the most impressive comes from the diary of Nicholas Motovilov, who as a young man came to Sarov seeking advice. At a certain point in their conversation, Seraphim said to his guest, "Look at me." Motovilov replied, "I am not able, Father, for there is lightning flashing in your eyes. Your face has grown more radiant than the sun and my eyes cannot bear the pain." The *staretz* answered, "Do not be afraid, my dear lover of God, you have also now become as radiant as I. You yourself are now in the fullness of the Holy Spirit. Otherwise you would not be able to perceive me in the exact same state." St. Seraphim asked him how he felt. "I feel a great calm in my soul, a peace which no words can express," Motovilov replied. "I feel an amazing happiness."[73]

At the heart of St. Seraphim's teaching was use of the Jesus Prayer and continuing inner struggle to "acquire the Holy Spirit, the one eternal treasure which will never pass away." He reassured those who came to him that there is nothing selfish about seeking to save your soul. "Acquire the Spirit of peace and thousands of souls around you will be saved."

Without a vital spiritual life, he said, we cannot love. "God is fire that warms and kindles the heart and inward parts. And so, if we feel in our hearts coldness, which is from the devil — for the devil is cold — then let us call upon the Lord and He will come and warm our hearts with perfect love not only for Him but for our neighbor as well."

He was an apostle of the way of love and kindness.

You cannot be too gentle, too kind. Shun even to appear harsh in your treatment of each other. Joy, radiant joy, streams from the face of him who gives and kindles joy in the heart of him who receives. All condemnation is from the devil. Never condemn each other. We condemn others only because we shun knowing ourselves. When we gaze at our own failings, we see such a swamp that nothing in another can equal it. That is why we turn away, and make much of the faults of others. Instead of condemning others, strive to reach inner peace. Keep silent, refrain from judgment. This will raise you above the deadly arrows of slander, insult and outrage and will shield your glowing hearts against all evil.

No matter what season of the year it was, he greeted visitors with the paschal salutation, "Christ is risen!" As another paschal gesture, he always wore a white robe.

On January 2, 1833, St. Seraphim was found dead in his cell, kneeling with hands crossed before an icon of Mary.

"St. Seraphim is a unique saint," Father Ghermann told me. "With St. Sergius, I think he is the most beloved saint in the Russian Church. Believers venerate him wholeheartedly. In him and his character, in his spirituality, we find the principal Christian characteristics — love for all people without exception, and a readiness to sacrifice. That's why people love him so much."

"We live in a time that pays special homage to advanced education and intellectual brilliance," Father Ghermann added. "But faith isn't just for the clever. Seraphim didn't graduate either from university or seminary. All his ideals were gifts from God revealed through prayer and deeds. And so through St. Seraphim many different people are drawn to belief—the intellectuals, the simple, and now not only people in the Russian Orthodox Church but other churches."

Before his death, St. Seraphim said to the sisters at Diveyevo: "My joys, come as often as you can to my grave. Come to me as if I'm alive and tell me everything, and I will always help you."

"St. Seraphim *is* the face of the Church," said Father Ghermann.

Living in a period in which iconography had been influenced by Western art, old icons of St. Seraphim often resemble portraits, while more recently made icons are usually in the simpler, more symbolic Byzantine style. The one reproduced on page 132 showing St. Seraphim praying on the rock was made in 1992 by the iconographer Philip Zimmerman closely following an icon made earlier in the century in France by the monk Gregory Kroug. In all icons of St. Seraphim, there is a prayer rope in his hands, a reminder of his devotion to the Jesus Prayer.

Holy Fools

*But God has chosen the foolish things of the world to con-
found the wise, and God has chosen the weak things of the
world to confound those who are mighty.*

— 1 CORINTHIANS 1:27

Few taunts are sharper than those that call into question someone's sanity: "He's crazy. He's a fool. He's an idiot. He's out
of touch. He's missing a few nuts and bolts. He isn't playing
with a full deck. There are bats in his belfry." Yet there are
saints whose acts of witness to the Gospel fly in the face of
what most of us regard as sanity. The Russian Church has a special word for such saints, *yurodivi*, meaning holy fools or fools
for Christ's sake. These are people in whom Christ wears the
disguise of madness.

While there is much variety among them, the holy fools
are in every case ascetic Christians living well outside the borders of conventional social behavior, including conventional
religious behavior. They are people who in most parts of the
developed world would be locked away in asylums or simply ig-
nored until the elements silenced them, after which they would
be thrown into unmarked graves.

While this type of saint is chiefly associated with Eastern
Christianity, the Western Church also has its holy fools. Perhaps Francis of Assisi is chief among them. Think of him
stripping off his clothes and standing naked before the bishop
in Assisi's main square, or preaching to birds, or taming a wolf,
or — during the Crusades — walking unarmed across the Egyptian desert into the Sultan's camp. What at first may seem like
charming scenes, when placed on the rough surface of actual
life, become mad moments indeed.

Perhaps there is a sense in which each and every saint, even
those who were scholars, would be regarded as insane by many
in the modern world because of their devotion to a way of

life that was completely senseless apart from the Gospel. Every saint is troubling. Every saint reveals some of our fears and makes us question our fear-driven choices.

The holy fool is not confined to the calendar of saints. In Dostoevsky's *Crime and Punishment,* we find a holy fool in Lizaveta, one of the two women murdered by Raskolnikov. She is simple minded but a pure soul, in contrast to her killer, a scholar intelligent enough to devise a philosophical justification for murder. (The name Dostoevsky assigns to his anti-hero Raskolnikov means someone cut off from the whole, a man out of communion.)

"Were you friends with Lizaveta?" Raskolnikov asks the prostitute Sonya. "Yes," Sonya responds. "She and I used to read and talk. She will see God."

Dostoevsky continues: "How strange these bookish words sounded to him; and here was another new thing: some sort of mysterious get-togethers with Lizaveta —two holy fools."

"One might well become a holy fool oneself here," exclaims Raskolnikov. "It's catching!"[74]

In Leo Tolstoy's memoir of his childhood, he recalls Grisha, a holy fool who sometimes wandered about his parent's estate and even into the mansion itself. "He gave little icons to those he took a fancy to," Tolstoy remembered. Among the local gentry, some regarded Grisha as a pure soul whose presence was a blessing, while others dismissed him as a lazy peasant. "I will only say one thing," Tolstoy's mother said at table one night, opposing her husband's view that Grisha should be put in prison. "It is hard to believe that a man, though he is sixty, goes barefoot summer and winter and always under his clothes wears chains weighing seventy pounds, and who has more than once declined a comfortable life...it is hard to believe that such a man does all this merely because he is lazy."[75]

Grisha, Lizaveta, and Sonya represent the rank-and-file of Russia's *yurodivi,* and one still finds them in Russia today. Few such men and women will be canonized, but nonetheless they help save those around them. They are reminders of God's presence.

The most famous of Russia's holy fools was a Muscovite, St. Basil the Blessed, after whom the colorful cathedral on Red

Square takes its name. In an ancient icon housed in that church, Basil is shown clothed only in his beard and a loin cloth. In the background is the Savior Tower and the churches packed within the Kremlin walls. Basil's hands are raised in prayer toward a small image of Jesus revealed in an opening in the sky. The holy fool has a meek quality but a single-minded, intelligent face. (*See color section.*)

It is hard to find the actual man beneath the thicket of tales and legends that grew up around his memory, but according to tradition Basil was clairvoyant from an early age. Thus, while a cobbler's apprentice, he both laughed and wept when a certain merchant ordered a pair of boots, for Basil saw that the man would be wearing a coffin before his new boots were ready. We can imagine that the merchant was not amused at the boy's behavior. Soon after — perhaps having been fired by the cobbler — Basil became a vagrant. Dressed as if for the Garden of Eden, Basil's survival of many bitter Russian winters must be reckoned among the miracles associated with his life.

A naked man wandering the streets — it isn't surprising that he became famous in the capital city. Especially for the wealthy, he was not a comfort either to eye or ear. In the eyes of some, he was a trouble-maker. There are tales of him destroying the merchandise of dishonest tradesmen at the market on Red Square. At times he hurled stones at the houses of the wealthy — yet, as if reverencing icons, he sometimes kissed the stones on the outside of houses in which evil had been committed, as if to say that no matter what happens within these walls, there is still hope of conversion.

Basil was one of the few who dared warn Tsar Ivan the Terrible that his violent deeds were dooming him to hell.

According to one story, in the midst of Lent, when Russians keep a rigorous vegetarian fast, Basil presented the tsar with a slab of raw beef, telling him that there was no reason in his case not to eat meat. "Why abstain from meat when you murder men?"[76] Basil asked. Ivan, whose irritated glance was a death sentence to others, is said to have lived in dread of Basil and would allow no harm to be done to him. Occasionally Ivan even sent gifts to the naked prophet of the streets, but Basil kept none of these for himself. Most that he received he gave to beggars, though in one surprising case a gift of gold from the tsar was passed on to a merchant. Others imagined the man was well off, but Basil discerned the man had been ruined and was actually starving but was too proud to beg.

Once Basil poured vodka, another royal gift, on the street; he wanted, he said, to put out the fires of sin.

Basil was so revered by Muscovites that, when he died, his thin body was buried, not in a pauper's grave on the city's edge, but next to the newly erected Cathedral of the Protection of the Mother of God. The people began to call the church St. Basil's, for to go there meant to pray at Basil's grave. Not many years passed before Basil was formally canonized by the Russian Church. A chapel built over his grave became an integral part of the great building, adding one more onion dome to the eight already there.[77]

Another fool for Christ was the heir to Ivan the Terrible's imperial throne, Tsar Theodore. Regarded by Western diplomats of the time as a weakling and idiot, Theodore was adored by the Russian people. Brought up in an environment of brutality, reviled by his father, regarded with scorn by courtiers, he became a man of simplicity, prayer, and quiet devotion to his wife. Much of his time was spent in church. It is said that throughout his fourteen years as tsar he never lost his playfulness or love of beauty. He sometimes woke the people of Moscow in the hours before dawn by sounding the great bells of the Kremlin, a summons to prayer. "He was small of stature," according to a contemporary account, "and bore the marks of fasting. He was humble, given to the things of the soul, constant in prayer, liberal in alms. He did not care for the things of this world, only for the salvation of the soul."[78]

"This simpleton," writes Nicholas Zernov, "robed in gorgeous vestments, was determined that bloodshed, cruelty and oppression must be stopped, and it was stopped as long as he occupied the throne of his ancestors."

In June 1988, I was present at a Church Council at the Holy Trinity–St. Sergius Lavra north of Moscow for the canonization of someone very like Basil and Theodore: St. Xenia of St. Petersburg.

Early in her long life Xenia had been married to an army colonel who drank himself to death and who may have been an abusive, violent husband. Soon after his funeral, she began giving away the family fortune to the poor, a simple act of obedience to Christ's teaching: "If you would be perfect, go, sell what you have and give it to the poor...and come, follow me." In order to prevent Xenia from impoverishing herself, relatives sought to have her declared insane. However the doctor who examined her concluded Xenia was the sanest person he had ever met.

Having given away her wealth, for some years Xenia disappeared, becoming one of Russia's many pilgrims walking from shrine to shrine while reciting the Jesus Prayer. Somewhere along the way during those hidden years, she became a fool for Christ. When Xenia finally returned to St. Petersburg, she was wearing the threadbare remnants of her late husband's military uniform — these are usually shown in the icons of her — and would answer only to his name, not her own. One can only guess her motives. In taking upon herself his name and clothing, she may have been attempting to do penance for his sins. Her home became the Smolensk cemetery on the city's edge where she slept rough year-round and where finally she was buried.

Xenia became known for her clairvoyant gift of telling people what to expect and what they should do, though what she said often made sense only in the light of later events. She might say to certain persons she singled out, "Go home and make blini [Russian pancakes]." As blini are served after funerals, the person she addressed would understand that a member of the family would soon die.

She never begged. Money was given to her, but she kept only an occasional kopek for herself; everything else was passed on to others.

When she died, age seventy-one, at the end of the eighteenth century, her grave became a place of pilgrimage and remained so even through the Soviet period, though for several decades the political authorities closed the chapel at her grave site. The official canonization of this fool for Christ and the reopening of the chapel over her grave were vivid gestures in the

St. Xenia of St. Petersburg, a "holy fool."

Gorbachev years that the war against religion was truly over in Russia.[79]

Why does the Church occasionally canonize people whose lives are not only completely at odds with civil society but who often hardly fit ecclesiastical society either? The answer must be that holy fools dramatize something about God that most Christians find embarrassing but that we vaguely recognize is crucial information.

It is the special vocation of holy fools to live out in a rough, literal, breathtaking way the "hard sayings" of Jesus. Like the Son of Man, they have no place to lay their heads, and, again like him, they live without money in their pockets (thus Jesus, in responding to a question about paying taxes, had no coin of his own with which to display Caesar's image). While never harming anyone, holy fools raise their voices against those who lie and cheat and do violence to others, but at the same time they are always ready to embrace these same greedy and ruth-less people. They take everyone seriously. No one, absolutely no one, is unimportant. In fact, the only thing always important for them, apart from God, saints, and angels, are the people around them, whoever they are, no matter how limited they are. Their dramatic gestures, however shocking, always have to do with revealing the person of Christ and his mercy.

For most people, clothing serves as a message of how high they have risen and how secure — or insecure — they are. Holy fools wear the wrong clothes, or rags, or perhaps nothing at all. This is a witness that they have nothing to lose. There is noth-ing to cling to and nothing for anyone to steal. The fool for Christ, says Bishop Kallistos of Diokleia, "has no possessions, no family, no position, and so can speak with a prophetic bold-ness. He cannot be exploited, for he has no ambition; and he fears God alone."[80]

The rag-dressed (or undressed) holy fool is like Issa, the wan-dering Japanese poet, who enjoyed possessing only what could not be taken away: "The thief left it behind! The moon in the window." Inevitably, the voluntary destitution and absolute vulnerability of the holy fool challenge us with our locks and keys and schemes to outwit destitution, suffering, and death.

Holy fools may be people of lesser intelligence, or quite brilliant. In the latter case such a follower of Christ may have found his or her path to foolishness as a way of overcoming pride and a need for recognition of intellectual gifts or spiritual attainments. The scholar of Russian spirituality George Fedotov points out that for all who seek mystical heights by following the traditional path of rigorous self-denial, there is always the problem of vainglory, "a great danger for monastic asceticism."[81] For such people a feigned madness, provoking from many others contempt or vilification, saves them from something worse: being honored. (One thinks of Dorothy Day's barbed comment: "Don't call me a saint — I don't want to be dismissed so easily.")

Clearly holy fools challenge an understanding of Christianity, more typical in Western than Eastern Christianity, that gives the intellectually gifted people a head start not only in economic efforts but spiritual life. But the Gospel and sacramental life aren't just for smart people. At the Last Judgment we will not be asked how clever we were but how merciful. Our academic ability won't save us. (In the Western Church, beginning in the Middle Ages, the idea took hold that sacramental life presupposed the life of reason and the ability to explain one's faith. Thus in the West children below "the age of reason," along with the deaf, the mute, and mentally retarded, were barred from communion.)

In their outlandish behavior, holy fools pose the question: Are we keeping heaven at a distance by clinging to the good regard of others, prudence, and what those around us regard as "sanity"? The holy fools shout out with their mad words and deeds that to seek God is not necessarily the same thing as to seek sanity.

We need to think long and hard about sanity, a word most of us cling to with a steel grip. Does fear of being regarded by others as insane confine me in a cage of "responsible" behavior that limits my freedom and cripples my ability to love? And is it in fact such a wonderful thing to be regarded as sane? After all, the chief administrator of the Holocaust, Adolf Eichmann, was declared "quite sane" by the psychiatrists who examined him before his trial in Jerusalem. Surely the same psychiatrists would have found St. Basil, St. Theodore, and St. Xenia all in-sane — and St. Francis, and that most revered of all madmen, the Son of Man, the Savior, Jesus of Nazareth.

Henry David Thoreau, by no means the most conventional man of his time, lamented on his death bed, "What demon possessed me that I behaved so well?" He would have taken comfort in holy fools. They remind us of a deeper sanity that is sometimes hidden beneath apparent lunacy: the treasure of a God-centered life.

Holy fools like St. Xenia are God-obsessed people who throw into the bonfire anything that gets in the way or leads them down blind alleys. But where does their path actually lead them? It is easier to say where they are *not* headed and what they are *not* taking with them than to describe where they are going. One can use a phrase like "the kingdom of God," but this reveals no more about what it is to live in the Holy Spirit than a dictionary entry on oranges reveals about the taste of an orange.

But were at least some of the holy fools, after all, not crazy? The answer must be, maybe so. While the fools for Christ who have been canonized are regarded by the Church as having worn madness as a mask, in fact no one knows how much a mask it really was, only that Christ shone through their lives. As Fedotov says, for most Russian people, "the difficulty [confronting many others] does not exist. Sincere [lunacy] or feigned, a madman with religious charisma ... is always a saint, perhaps the most beloved saint in Russia."[82]

Part V

Prayers of the Day

☦

Here is a short selection of prayers widely used in the Orthodox Church. Often such prayers would be recited in an "icon corner" in the home. In this version, "you" rather than "thee" is used in addressing God; the latter was once the more intimate form of address, but many now experience it not only as archaic but as more formal. An effort has been made to reduce the use of the masculine pronoun in referring to God or to men and women collectively. See the chapter "Praying in Body and Soul" (pp. 40–50) for further advice about praying with icons.

Morning Prayer

In the name of the Father and of the Son and of the Holy Spirit. Amen. [*whenever invoking the Holy Trinity, make the sign of the cross*]

Glory to you, our God, glory to you.

O Heavenly King, the Comforter, the Spirit of truth, everywhere present and filling all things, treasury of blessings and giver of life, come and dwell in us and cleanse us of every impurity and save our souls, O Holy One.

During the fifty days of the paschal season, in place of "O Heavenly King":

Christ is risen from the dead, trampling down death by death, and upon those in the tomb bestowing life.

Let God arise, and let his enemies be scattered, and let all those who hate him flee before him.

Christ is risen from the dead, trampling down death by death, and upon those in the tomb bestowing life.

As the smoke vanishes, so shall they vanish, and as wax melts before fire.

Christ is risen from the dead, trampling down death by death, and upon those in the tomb bestowing life.

Even so let those who hate God vanish before him, but let the righteous rejoice.

Christ is risen from the dead, trampling down death by death, and upon those in the tomb bestowing life.

This is the day the Lord has made. We will rejoice and be glad in it.

Christ is risen from the dead, trampling down death by death, and upon those in the tomb bestowing life.

Glory to the Father, and to the Son, and to the Holy Spirit.

Christ is risen from the dead, trampling down death by death,
and upon those in the tomb bestowing life.
Now and ever and unto ages of ages. Amen.
Christ is risen from the dead, trampling down death by death,
and upon those in the tomb bestowing life.

Holy God! Holy Mighty! Holy Immortal! Have mercy on us.
[*bow*]
Holy God! Holy Mighty! Holy Immortal! Have mercy on us.
[*bow*]
Holy God! Holy Mighty! Holy Immortal! Have mercy on us.
[*bow*]
Glory to the Father and to the Son and to the Holy Spirit, now
and ever and unto ages of ages. Amen.

O Most Holy Trinity, have mercy on us. O Lord, cleanse us from
our sins. O Master, pardon our transgressions. O Holy One, visit
and heal our infirmities for your name's sake.

Lord, have mercy. Lord, have mercy. Lord, have mercy.

Our Father in heaven, hallowed be your name. Your kingdom
come, your will be done, on earth as it is in heaven. Give us this
day our daily bread. And forgive us our trespasses, as we forgive
those who trespass against us. And lead us not into temptation,
but deliver us from the evil one.

Having risen from sleep, we fall down before you, O Blessed
One, and sing to you, O Mighty One, the angelic hymn: Holy,
Holy, Holy are you, O God. Through the Theotokos, have mercy
on us. Glory to the Father and to the Son and to the Holy Spirit.
Having raised me from my bed and from sleep, O Lord, enlighten my mind and heart and open my lips that I might praise
you, O Holy Trinity: Holy, Holy, Holy are you, O God. Through
the Theotokos, have mercy on us. Now and ever and unto ages
of ages. Amen. The Judge will come suddenly and the acts of
every person will be revealed. But in the middle of the night
we cry with fear: Holy, Holy, Holy are you, O God. Through
the Theotokos, have mercy on us.

Come, let us worship God our King. [*prostration except during the season of Pascha*]

Come, let us worship and fall down before Christ, our King and our God. [*prostration*]

Come, let us worship and fall down before Christ Himself, our King and our God. [*prostration*]

Psalm 3, Psalm 63 (or other psalms)

We praise, bless, hymn, and thank you for bringing us out of the shadows of night and showing us again the light of day. In your goodness we beg you, cleanse us from our sins and accept our prayer in your great tenderness of heart, for we run to you, the merciful and all-powerful God. Illumine our hearts with the true Sun of Righteousness; enlighten our minds and guard all our senses, that walking uprightly as in the day in the way of your commandments, we may attain eternal life. For with you is the fountain of life and we will be made worthy of enjoying your unapproachable light. For you are our God, and to you we ascribe glory: to the Father and to the Son and to the Holy Spirit, now and ever and unto ages of ages. Amen.

Psalm 148:
Praise the Lord!
Praise the Lord from the heavens.
Praise God, in the heights.
Praise God, all you angels.
Praise God, all you hosts.
Praise God, sun and moon.
Praise God, all you stars of light.
Praise God, you heavens of heavens,
and you waters above the heavens.

Let them praise the name of the Lord,
for God commanded and they were created,
God established them forever,
making a decree that will never pass away.

Praise the Lord from the earth,
you great sea creatures in all the depths,

fire and hail, snow and clouds,
stormy winds, fulfilling God's word,
mountains and hills,
fruit trees and cedars,
beasts and cattle,
creeping things and fowl of the air,
rulers of the earth and all peoples,
princes and all judges of the earth,
young men and maidens,
old men and children:
let them praise the name of the Lord,
for God's name alone is exalted,
God's glory is above earth and heaven.
God has exalted the horn of his people,
the praise of all his saints,
all the children of Israel,
a people dear to him.

Glory to God in the highest and on earth peace, goodwill toward all. We praise you, we bless you, we worship you, we glorify you, we give thanks to you for your great glory. O Lord God, Heavenly King, God the Father Almighty. O Lord, the only-begotten Son, Jesus Christ and the Holy Spirit. O Lord God, Lamb of God, Son of the Father, who take away the sin of the world, have mercy on us. You take away the sin of the world: receive our prayer. You sit at the right hand of God the Father: have mercy on us. For you alone are Holy, you alone are Lord, you alone, O Jesus Christ, are most high in the glory of God the Father. Amen.

Every day will I give thanks to you and praise your name for ever and ever.

Lord, you have been our refuge from generation to generation. I said: Lord, be merciful to me. Heal my soul for I have sinned against you. Lord, I flee to you. Teach me to do your will, for you are my God. With you is the fountain of life and in your light we shall see light. Continue your mercy to those who know you.

O Lord, keep us this day without sin.

Blessed are you, O Lord God, praised and glorified is your name
  forever. Amen.
Let your mercy, O Lord, be upon us as we have set our hope
  in you.
Blessed are you, O Lord, teach me your statutes.
Blessed are you, O Master, make me to understand your commandments.
Blessed are you, O Holy One, enlighten me with your precepts.
Your mercy, O Lord, endures forever. Do not despise the work
  of your hands.
To you belongs worship. To you belongs praise. To you belongs
  glory. To the Father and to the Son and to the Holy Spirit,
  now and ever and unto ages of ages. Amen.

Most Holy God, give each of us a pure heart and way of speaking that befits the faith we profess; grant us uprightness of
purpose, powers of reasoning unhindered by passions, conduct
that becomes those who fear you, and perfect knowledge of
your commandments. May we enjoy health in body and in
spirit. Grant us a life of peace, genuine faith and living hope,
sincere charity and bountiful generosity, patience that knows
no bounds and the light of your truth to proclaim your goodness to us, that for ever and in all things placing our trust only
in you, we may abound in every good work, and that in Christ
your gifts may increase in every soul. For to you belong all
glory, honor, and majesty, Father, Son, and Holy Spirit, now and
ever and unto ages of ages. Amen.

Hail, O Mother of God and Virgin Mary, full of grace, the Lord
is with you. Blessed are you among women and blessed is the
fruit of your womb, for you have borne the Savior of our souls.
More honorable than the cherubim and more glorious beyond
compare than the seraphim, without defilement you gave birth
to God the Word. True Mother of God, we magnify you.

  Beneath your tenderness of heart do we take refuge, O Theotokos. Despise not our appeals in our necessity, but from all
perils deliver us, O only pure, only blessed. Most glorious ever

virgin, Mother of Christ our God, bring our prayers to your Son and our God that he may for your sake save our souls.

Prayer of the Elders of Optino:
Lord, grant that I may meet the coming day with spiritual tranquility. Grant that in all things I may rely upon your holy will. In each hour of the day, reveal your will to me. Whatever news may reach me this day, teach me to accept it with a calm soul, knowing that all is subject to your holy will. Direct my thoughts and feelings in all my words and actions. In all unexpected occurrences, do not let me forget that all is sent down by you. Grant that I may deal firmly and wisely with every member of my family and all who are in my care, neither embarrassing nor saddening anyone. Give me the strength to bear the fatigue of the coming day with all that it shall bring. Direct my will and teach me to pray, to believe, to hope, to be patient, to forgive, and to love. Amen.

Glory to you, O Christ our God and our sure hope, glory to you.

Through the prayers of the Theotokos and of all the saints, Lord Jesus Christ our God, have mercy on us and save us. Amen.

A deacon singing before the iconostasis in St. Vladimir's
Cathedral, Kiev.

Evening Prayer

Everything from morning prayer until after the Our Father.
Alleluia, Alleluia, Alleluia. Glory to you, O God. [*bow*]
Alleluia, Alleluia, Alleluia. Glory to you, O God. [*bow*]
Alleluia, Alleluia, Alleluia. Glory to you, O God. [*bow*]

Psalm 141, Psalm 142, and Psalm 130

O Gladsome Light of the holy glory of the Immortal Father: heavenly, holy blessed Jesus Christ. Now that we have come to the setting of the sun and behold the light of evening, we praise God, Father, Son, and Holy Spirit, for good it is at all times to worship you with voices of praise, O Son of God and giver of life. Therefore the whole world glorifies you.

O Lord, be pleased to keep us this night without sin.

Blessed are you, Lord God of our Fathers, praised and glorified be your name forever. Amen.
Be merciful to us, O Lord, as we have set our hope in you.
Blessed are you, O Lord, teach me your statutes.
Blessed are you, O Master, make me to understand your commandments.
Blessed are you, O Holy One, enlighten me with your precepts.
Your mercy, O Lord, endures forever. Do not despise the work of your hands.
To you belongs worship, to you belongs praise, to you belongs glory.
To the Father and to the Son and to the Holy Spirit, now and ever and unto ages of ages.
Amen.

Psalm 123

Glory to the Father and to the Son and to the Holy Spirit, now and ever and unto ages of ages. Amen.

Prayer of St. Simeon:
Lord, now let your servant depart in peace, according to your word, for my eyes have seen your salvation, which you have prepared before the face of all peoples, a light to enlighten the Gentiles and to be the glory of your people Israel.

Rejoice, O Virgin Theotokos, Mary, full of grace, the Lord is with you. Blessed are you among women and blessed is the fruit of your womb, for you have borne the Savior of our souls. More honorable than the cherubim and more glorious beyond compare than the seraphim, without defilement you gave birth to God the Word. True Mother of God, we magnify you. Beneath your tenderness of heart do we take refuge, O Theotokos. Despise not our appeals in our necessity, but from all perils deliver us, O only pure, only blessed. Most glorious ever virgin, Mother of Christ our God, bring our prayers to your Son and our God that he may for your sake save our souls.

Glory to the Father and to the Son and to the Holy Spirit.

Compline _____

In the name of the Father, and of the Son, and of the Holy Spirit, now and ever and unto ages of ages. Amen.

Psalm 51

Glory to the Father and to the Son and to the Holy Spirit, now and ever and unto ages of ages. Amen.

I believe in one God, the Father Almighty, the Maker of heaven and earth, and of all things visible and invisible.

And in one Lord Jesus Christ, the Son of God, the Only-begotten, begotten of the Father before all ages. Light of Light; true God of true God; begotten not made; of one essence with the Father by whom all things were made; Who for us men and our salvation came down from heaven and was incarnate of the Holy Spirit and the Virgin Mary, and became man. And He was crucified for us under Pontius Pilate, and suffered and was buried. And the third day He rose again, according to the scriptures, and ascended into heaven, and sits at the right hand of the Father; and He shall come again to judge the living and the dead; whose kingdom will have no end.

And in the Holy Spirit, the Lord, the Giver of Life, who proceeds from the Father; who with the Father and the Son is worshiped and glorified; who spoke by the prophets.

In one Holy, Catholic, and Apostolic Church.

I acknowledge one baptism for the remission of sins. I look for the resurrection of the dead, and the life of the world to come. Amen.

Grant rest, Master, to our souls and bodies as we sleep; preserve us from the gloomy slumber of sin and from the dark passions of the night. Calm the impulses of carnal desires; quench the fiery darts of the evil one which are craftily directed against us.

Still the rebellions of the flesh and put far from us all anxiety and worldly cares.

Grant us, O God, a watchful mind, a sober heart, and a quiet rest, free from every vision of the devil. Raise us up again at the hour of prayer, strengthened in your precepts, and holding within us steadfastly the thought of your commandments.

Grant that we may sing praises to you through the night and that we may hymn, bless, and glorify your all-honorable and majestic name, of the Father, and of the Son, and of the Holy Spirit, now and ever and unto ages of ages. Amen.

Prayers
of Intercession

Forgive, O Lord, those who hate us and treat us unjustly. Do
good to those who do good.
Lord, have mercy.
Grant our brethren and families their requests which are for
salvation and eternal life.
Lord, have mercy.
Visit those who are ill and grant them healing.
Lord, have mercy.
Watch over those at sea and accompany those who travel.
Lord, have mercy.
Grant remission of sins to those who serve us and are kind
to us.
Lord, have mercy.
Grant guidance and wisdom to all those in public service.
Lord, have mercy.
Be merciful according to your great mercy to those who have
asked us to pray for them, unworthy though we be.
Lord, have mercy.
Remember, O Lord, our fathers, mothers, brothers, and sisters
who have fallen asleep before us and grant them rest where
the light of your countenance shines.
Lord, have mercy.
Remember, O Lord, those who are in captivity and deliver them
from every distress.
Lord, have mercy.
Remember, O Lord, those who bring offerings and do good in
your holy churches and grant them their requests which are
for salvation and eternal life.
Lord, have mercy.

Remember us, your sinful and unworthy servants, O Lord, and enlighten our minds with the light of your knowledge, guiding us along the way of your commandments, by the intercessions of your immaculate Mother, our Lady Theotokos and ever-virgin Mary, and of all your saints. For you are blessed unto ages of ages. Amen.

Lord have mercy. Lord have mercy. Lord have mercy.

Most glorious ever Virgin, Mother of Christ our God, bring our prayers to your Son and our God, that he for your sake may save our souls.

My hope is the Father, my refuge is the Son, my shelter is the Holy Spirit, O Holy Trinity, glory to you.

Have mercy on us, O Lord, have mercy on us, for we sinners who are without means of defense offer you our Master this supplication, have mercy on us.

Glory to the Father and to the Son and to the Holy Spirit.

Lord have mercy on us, for our trust is in you. Do not be angry with us and do not remember our sins, but look upon us now in your compassion and deliver us from our enemies. For you are our God and we are your people. We are all the work of your hands and we call upon your name, now and ever and unto ages of ages. Amen.

Open the doors of your loving-kindness to us, O blessed Mother of God, that we who put our hope in you may not fail. Through you may we be delivered from adversities, for you are the salvation of the Christian family.

Most holy Theotokos, save us. More honorable than the cherubim and beyond compare more glorious than the seraphim. Without defilement you gave birth to God the Word. True Theotokos, we magnify you.

Glory to you, O Christ our God and our sure hope, glory to you.

Glory to the Father and to the Son and to the Holy Spirit, now and ever and unto ages of ages. Amen.

Through the prayers of our holy Fathers, O Lord Jesus Christ our God, have mercy on us and save us. Amen.

The Litany of Peace _____

This series of short petitions, from the first part of the Liturgy, can be used at any time.

In peace let us pray to the Lord.
Lord have mercy.
For the peace from above and for the salvation of our souls, let us pray to the Lord.
Lord have mercy.
For the peace of the whole world, for the welfare of the holy churches of God, and for the union of all, let us pray to the Lord.
Lord have mercy.
For this holy house and for those who enter with faith, reverence, and the fear of God, let us pray to the Lord.
Lord have mercy.
For this city, for every city and country, and for the faithful dwelling in them, let us pray to the Lord.
Lord have mercy.
For seasonable weather, for abundance of the fruits of the earth and for peaceful times, let us pray to the Lord.
Lord have mercy.
For travelers by land, by sea, and by air, for the sick and the suffering; for prisoners and their salvation, let us pray to the Lord.
Lord have mercy.
For our deliverance from all affliction, wrath, danger, and necessity, let us pray to the Lord.
Lord have mercy.
Help us, save us, have mercy on us, and keep us, O God, by your grace.
Lord have mercy.

Commemorating our most glorious, most pure, most blessed and glorious Lady, Mother of God and ever-virgin Mary, let us commend ourselves and each other and all our life unto Christ our God.

To you, O Lord.

Obtaining Icons
or Icon Prints

You are likely to find a selection of icon prints, mounted and unmounted, for sale at any local Orthodox parish. Certainly there will be people there ready to help you.

Hand-painted icons are less easy to find, except at hugely inflated prices in certain art galleries, but in local Orthodox parishes you may find a skilled iconographer as well as advice about monasteries whose members include iconographers able to accept commissions.

Increasingly icon prints are sold in religious bookshops.

Here is a short list of places in the United States, Britain, and the Netherlands I know of personally, or have been told of by friends, through which good icon prints are available. My apologies to the many churches, monasteries, communities, and shops that are not included.

In the United States

St. Vladimir's Seminary Bookstore
575 Scarsdale Road
Crestwood, NY 10707–1699
toll-free tel: (800) 204–2665
tel: (914) 961–2203
fax: (914) 961–5456
e-mail: bookstore@svots.attmail.com

Holy Cross Orthodox Bookstore
50 Goddard Avenue
Brookline, MA 02146
tel: (800) 245–0599

St. Isaac of Syria Skete
Route 1, Box 168
Boscobel, WI 53805
toll-free tel: (800) 814–2667
tel: (608) 375–5500
fax: (608) 375–5555
e-mail: stisaacske@aol.com

Oakwood Publications
3827 Bluff Street
Torrance, CA 90505–6359
toll-free tel: (800) 747–9245

Dormition Skete Icons
PO Box 3177
Buena Vista, CO 81211
tel: (719) 395–8898

Holy Transfiguration Monastery
278 Warren Street
Brookline, MA 02146–5997
toll-free tel: (800) 227–1629

Conciliar Press
PO Box 76
Ben Lomond, CA 95005–0076
toll-free tel: (800) 967–7377
tel: (408) 336–5118

St. Herman of Alaska Bookstore
1315 7th Avenue
San Francisco, CA 94122
tel: (415) 664–8161

Holy Virgin Cathedral Bookstore
6200 Geary Boulevard
San Francisco, CA 94121
tel: (415) 668–5218

In Great Britain

Cathedral of the Dormition of the Mother
of God and All Saints
67 Ennismore Gardens
London SW7 1NH
tel: (0171) 584–0096

Monastery of St John the Baptist
Rectory Road
Tolleshunt Knights
Malden, Essex CM9 8E2
tel: (0621) 816–471

Barnabas and Alexandra Wilson
23 Brimley Vale
Bovey Tracey
Devon TQ13 9DA
tel: (01626) 832–770

In the Netherlands

Orthodox Information Center
St. Nicholas of Myra Russian Orthodox Church
Kerkstraat 342
1017 JA Amsterdam
tel: (020) 421–1815

Notes

1. For more about the place of iconography in Merton's life see "The Christ of the Icons," in Jim Forest, *Living with Wisdom: A Biography of Thomas Merton* (Maryknoll, N.Y.: Orbis Books, 1991), 23–28.

2. Maxim Gorky, *My Childhood*, trans. Ronald Wilks (London: Penguin Classics, 1966), 100–101; the same book contains a description, no less remarkable, of his grandmother's evening prayers (60–61).

3. The text is included at the end of the Daily Prayer section of this book (p. 161).

4. Eusebius, *The History of the Church*, chap. 7, section 18.

5. Among guide books to Rome that draw special attention to ancient Christian art, one of the best is S. G. A. Luff, *The Christian's Guide to Rome* (Tunbridge Wells, England: Burns & Oates; first published 1967, revised edition 1990).

6. St. John of Damascus, *On the Divine Images* (Crestwood, N.Y.: St. Vladimir's Seminary Press, 1980).

7. Both icons by St. Andrei Rublev are part of the collection at the Tretyakov Gallery in Moscow.

8. "The Meaning and Language of Icons," an essay in Leonid Ouspensky and Vladimir Lossky, *The Meaning of Icons* (Crestwood, N.Y.: St. Vladimir's Seminary Press, 1982).

9. Vladimir Ivanov, *Russian Icons* (New York: Rizzoli, 1988), 181.

10. From Thomas Merton's as yet unpublished book, *Art and Worship*. It was to have gone to press in 1959; the galley sheets survive at the Thomas Merton Study Center at Bellarmine College in Louisville along with correspondence about the ill-fated project. Several correspondents struggled unsuccessfully to bring Merton up-to-date on the subject of religious art. The art historian Eloise Spaeth was enlisted to help ferry Merton's aesthetic judgment into the modern world, but in the end she despaired of the project. She was appalled with Merton's " 'sacred artist' who keeps creeping out with his frightful icons." For details about *Art and Worship*, see Donna Kristoff's essay, "Light That Is Not Light: A Consideration of Thomas Merton and the Icon," *The Merton Annual* 2 (New York: A. M. S. Press, 1989): 85–117.

11. Ouspensky and Lossky, *The Meaning of Icons*, 48–49.

12. Paul Evdokimov, *The Art of the Icon: A Theology of Beauty* (Redondo Beach, Calif.: Oakwood Publications, 1992), 236.

13. For a detailed study of inverse perspective, see Egon Sendler, S.J., *The Icon, Image of the Invisible: Elements of Theology, Aesthetics and Technique* (Redondo Beach, Calif.: Oakwood Publications, 1988), 119–48.

14. Ouspensky and Lossky, *The Meaning of Icons*, 27.

15. Ibid., 43.

16. Letters to June Jungblut, June 22, 1967, and March 29, 1968; reprinted in William H. Shannon, ed., *The Hidden Ground of Love: The Letters*

of Thomas Merton on Religious Experience and Social Concerns (New York: Farrar Straus & Giroux, 1985), 637, 642–43.

17. See Michael Gough, *The Origins of Christian Art* (London: Thames & Hudson, 1973).

18. For a detailed description of this process as well as every other step in making an icon, see Daniel V. Thompson, Jr., *The Practice of Tempera Painting* (New York: Dover Publications, 1963).

19. Ouspensky and Lossky, *The Meaning of Icons,* 54.

20. M. V. Alpatov, *Early Russian Icon Painting* (Moscow: Iskusstvo Press, 1978), 23.

21. This text, of unknown origin, is reprinted from *An Iconographer's Patternbook: The Straganov Tradition* (Torrance, Calif.: Oakwood Publications, 1992).

22. W. H. Auden, "Prayer, Nature Of" in *A Certain World* (1970).

23. Alexander Schmemann, "Worship in a Secular Age," in *For the Life of the World,* rev. ed. (Crestwood, N.Y.: St. Vladimir's Seminary Press, 1973), 117-35.

24. John Donne, *Eighty Sermons,* no. 80, sct. 3; the sermon was preached December 12, 1626.

25. From the memoirs of Daniel Wheeler, published in England in 1842 and noted in Richenda Scott's book, *Quakers and Russia.* I am indebted to Peter Jarman, a Quaker who worked in Russia for several years, for drawing my attention to this story.

26. Metropolitan Anthony of Sourozh, *The Essence of Prayer* (London: Darton, Longman & Todd, 1989), 181–82. This section of the book was also published separately as *School for Prayer.*

27. Metropolitan Anthony of Sourozh, *The Essence of Prayer,* 186–87.

28. Dogmatic Poems, *Patrologia Graeca,* 37, 311–14, as cited in Olivier Clément, *The Roots of Christian Mysticism* (London: New City, 1993), 193–94.

29. Iulia de Beausobre, *Macarius, Starets of Optino: Russian Letters of Spiritual Direction* (London: Dacre Press, 1944), 87.

30. Chrismation, one the sacraments in the Orthodox Church, is similar to Confirmation in the Roman Catholic Church. In this rite, the sign of the cross is made with myrrh on various parts of the body: forehead, eyes, lips, ears, hands, and feet.

31. "The Merton Tapes," tape 8, side B, "Life and Solitude," a talk given in 1965 (Louisville: Bellarmine College, The Thomas Merton Studies Center).

32. For further reading, see *The Jesus Prayer,* by A Monk of the Eastern Church [Father Lev Gillet] (Crestwood, N.Y.: St. Vladimir's Seminary Press, 1987); and Bishop Kallistos of Diokleia, *The Power of the Name* (Fairacres, Oxford: Convent of the Incarnation, 1986).

33. There is a very similar Orthodox prayer: "Hail, O Mother of God and Virgin Mary, full of grace, the Lord is with you. Blessed are you among women and blessed is the fruit of your womb, for you have borne Jesus, the Savior of our souls."

34. Doreen Bartholomew, one of the pre-publication readers of this book, made the comment: "Here in the USA a person can be literally persecuted for being religious. Many companies forbid religious symbols on desks

or, when visible, on the persons themselves. Crosses must be concealed under clothing."

35. A Monk of the Eastern Church [Father Lev Gillet], *The Year of Grace of the Lord: A Scriptural and Liturgical Commentary on the Calendar of the Orthodox Church* (Crestwood, N.Y.: St. Vladimir's Seminary Press, 1980), 1.

36. Ouspensky and Lossky, *The Meaning of Icons,* 27.

37. Ibid., 27.

38. The term comes from the Latin word for almond.

39. Cited in Ouspensky and Lossky, *The Meaning of Icons,* 172.

40. Divine Names, IV, 2 (*Patrologia Graeca,* 3, 969); cited in Clément, *The Roots of Christian Mysticism,* 222.

41. A nearly identical icon is found in the Cathedral of the Archangel Michael within the Moscow Kremlin.

42. *The Festal Menaion,* translated from the Greek by Mother Mary and Archimandrite Kallistos Ware (London: Faber & Faber, 1969), 252.

43. Gillet, *The Year of Grace of the Lord,* 82.

44. See Father Steven Bigham, *The Image of God the Father in Orthodox Theology and Iconography* (Torrance, Calif.: Oakwood Publications, 1995).

45. One area of division between churches has to do with the calendar. Most of the Orthodox world uses the "old" or Julian calendar, which is thirteen days behind the "new" or Gregorian calendar, used by all Western churches and serving throughout the world as the calendar of secular life. Churches in Russia, for example, would celebrate Theophany on January 19, as reckoned by the new calendar.

46. Schmemann, *For the Life of the World,* 131–32.

47. Bishop Kallistos Ware, *The Orthodox Way,* rev. ed. (Crestwood, N.Y.: St. Vladimir's Seminary Press, 1995), 127.

48. Ouspensky and Lossky, *The Meaning of Icons,* 211.

49. *Patrologia Graeca,* 151, 433 B; cited in Evdokimov, *The Art of the Icon,* 233.

50. "Homily on the Presentation of the Blessed Virgin in the Temple."

51. Note that the Greek verb παραδίδωμι, is often mistranslated as "to betray"; see William Klassen, *Judas: Betrayer or Friend of Jesus?* (Minneapolis: Augsburg Fortress Press, 1996), chap. 3.

52. The word comes from the Hebrew word *Pesach,* for Passover. The Indo-European root for Easter is *aus,* to shine, and is linked with the goddess of dawn.

53. Text from the Holy Liturgy on the Sunday of the Myrrh-Bearing Women, the third Sunday of the Pascha season.

54. The bishop of Rome, inheriting Peter's place in the apostolic community, is still regarded by Orthodox Christians as having a place of special honor, but Orthodoxy, in its stress on conciliarity, objects to any form of monarchism in the episcopal office.

55. Evdokimov, *The Art of the Icon,* 246.

56. It is presently in the Tretyakov Gallery in Moscow.

57. Quoted by Sergei Averuntsev, "Beauty, Sanctity and Truth," *UNESCO Courier,* June 1988.

58. Ouspensky and Lossky, *The Meaning of Icons,* 213–15.

59. Gillet, *The Year of Grace of the Lord,* 244.

60. Sergius Bulgakov, *The Orthodox Church* (Crestwood, N.Y.: St. Vladimir's Seminary Press, 1988), 116–17.

61. Paula Bowes, "Mary and the Early Church Fathers," *Epiphany,* special issue on Mary the Theotokos (Summer 1984): 46.

62. David Crystal, "The Whole Story," in *The Cambridge Encyclopedia of the English Language* (Cambridge: Cambridge University Press, 1995), 22.

63. On the Dormition of the Virgin, *Patrologia Graeca,* 151, 468 A B.

64. Henri Nouwen, *Behold the Beauty of the Lord: Praying with Icons* (Notre Dame, Ind.: Ave Maria Press, 1987), 36.

65. Thomas Merton, *The Ascent to Truth* (New York: Harcourt Brace & Co., 1951), 317.

66. The principal ancient text about Sts. Anne and Joachim, neither of whom is mentioned in the New Testament, is a second-century text, the *Protoevangelium* of St. James. "It must be pointed out that the historical evidence on which the legend is based is by no means satisfactory," comments one of the authors of *The Saints,* "but it is to be remembered that the legitimacy and authenticity of the devotion depend on the approval of the church, which it possesses, and not on the legendary account of its origins." It is noteworthy that God has blessed those who have invoked the grandparents of Jesus with many miracles (John Coulson et al., eds., *The Saints* [Guild], 691).

67. Megan McKenna's book *Angels Unawares* (Maryknoll, N.Y.: Orbis Books, 1995) is a good introduction to angels.

68. From the foreword to *Demons* by Fyodor Dostoevsky, a new translation by Richard Pevear and Larissa Volokhonsky (New York: Knopf, 1994), xiv.

69. This was not baptism into the Church, which would become after Pentecost a fundamental sacrament of Christianity, but rather a symbolic washing away of sins as a sign of repentance.

70. The distinctive vestment of bishops in the Orthodox Church always worn during services, similar to the *pallium* worn by bishops in the West.

71. For a detailed biographical study, see Pierre Kovalevsky's *Saint Sergius and Russian Spirituality* (Crestwood, N.Y.: St. Vladimir's Seminary Press, 1976).

72. *Staretz,* the Russian word for elder, has come to mean a person with a rare spiritual authority arising from the inner life of the elder himself, enabling him to provide spiritual direction to many people, even though they may be strangers. Dostoevsky, in *The Brothers Karamazov,* portrays such a person in the character of Father Zosima.

73. The full text of Motovilov's conversation with St. Seraphim, found and published only after St. Seraphim's canonization in 1903, is included in *A Treasury of Russian Spirituality,* compiled and edited by George Fedotov, first published in 1950 by Sheed & Ward and reissued in 1975 by Nordland. I am aware of two biographies of the *staretz* in English: Valentine Zander, *St. Seraphim of Sarov* (Crestwood, N.Y.: St. Vladimir's Seminary Press, 1975), and Iulia de Beausobre, *Flame in the Snow* (London: Collins, 1945, reissued as a Fount paperback in 1979). A collection of the saint's writings has been published in English as the first volume of *The Little Russian Philokalia: St. Seraphim* (Platina, Calif.: St. Herman of Alaska Monastery Press, 1991).

74. Fyodor Dostoevsky, *Crime and Punishment,* trans. Richard Pevear and Larissa Volokhonsky (New York: Knopf, 1992). One of the many strengths of

this edition is that the translators understand the significance of Dostoevsky's use of the word *yurodivi.*

75. Leo Tolstoy, *Childhood, Boyhood and Youth* (Oxford: Oxford University Press, 1928), 27–28.

76. This event is also attributed to the Holy Fool Nicholas of Pskov.

77. Some of the material about Blessed Basil's life comes from an essay on "The Holy Fools" in George P. Fedotov's *The Russian Religious Mind,* vol. 2 (Belmont, Mass.: Nordland Press, 1975); see esp. 337–39.

78. "A Brief Description of the Moscow Czars, of Their Appearance, Age, Habits and Disposition," quoted by Nicolas Zernov in *The Russians and Their Church,* 3d ed. (Crestwood, N.Y.: St. Vladimir's Seminary Press, 1978), 66–67.

79. Most of what I have learned about St. Xenia was told to me by people I met in St. Petersburg and heard at her canonization. There is very little about her in English. The only text I know of is a booklet, *The Life and Miracles of Blessed Xenia of St. Petersburg* (Jordanville, N.Y.: Holy Trinity Monastery, 1973).

80. Bishop Kallistos, "The Fool in Christ as Prophet and Apostle," *Sobornost* 6, no. 2 (1984). *Sobornost* is the quarterly magazine of the Fellowship of St. Alban and St. Sergius, 1 Canterbury Rd., Oxford OX2 6LU, England.

81. Fedotov, "The Holy Fools," *The Russian Religious Mind,* 319.

82. Ibid., 324.